THE HOUSE ALWAYS WINS

Time to Turn the Tables

THE HOUSE ALWAYS WINS

Time to Turn the Tables

JOHN McGUINNESS TD ∾
and
NAOISE NUNN ∾

Gill & Macmillan

Gill & Macmillan Ltd
Hume Avenue, Park West, Dublin 12
with associated companies throughout the world
www.gillmacmillan.ie

© John McGuinness and Naoise Nunn 2010
978 07171 4789 2

Typography design by Make Communication
Print origination by Carole Lynch
Printed and bound in the UK by CPI Mackays, Chatham ME5 8TD

This book is typeset in Linotype Minion and
Neue Helvetica.

The paper used in this book comes from the wood
pulp of managed forests. For every tree felled, at least
one tree is planted, thereby renewing natural
resources.

A CIP catalogue record for this book is available from
the British Library.

5 4 3 2 1

To my family for their forbearance, love and care, and to Kilkenny and its people, the bedrock of my beliefs.

CONTENTS

INTRODUCTION

On the morning of 22 April 2009, I got a call that was certainly not welcome but was not entirely unexpected. Brian Cowen was on the line to tell me that I would not be re-appointed as Minister of State for Trade and Commerce. The conversation was brief; by then Brian and I knew where we stood with one another. He said he wouldn't be re-appointing me. I said: 'OK' and that was it. I believed I had been doing a good job—I certainly worked diligently at it—but my stance, both inside and outside the Department, regarding inefficiencies, State indifferences and bad management had ensured that senior civil servants, my Minister, Mary Coughlan, and trade union officials were not exactly Facebook friends. This, added to a growing and obvious concern about Brian Cowen's ability to lead, would have militated against my re-appointment.

There is a price to be paid for speaking out and politicians should always be ready to pay it. It is better to stand up and fight for what you believe in than sit in office with your backbone broken. I am a conviction politician. There is so much I want to do, things I want to say, questions I want to ask, solutions I want to propose and debates I want to encourage and participate in. Doing that as Minister cost me my job, but I also received a huge amount of encouragement and support from the public: confirmation that they too want change.

I have 30 years' experience as a politician and I know the systems and culture of the State intimately. I know that change is needed and must happen. I have my opinions about that and my views on how we as a people can make a better future. I have been persuaded that writing a book about all of this would be worthwhile. I hope that is the case, because while writing it I have had frequent conversations with myself about vanity, values and vision. In the end, I think I feel better about writing it than I would be about staying silent.

This has nothing to do with sour grapes—I have nothing to be sour about. I did what I felt I had to do and I understood the price. I follow my father's advice to leave grudges behind and move on. This book was written because we need to radically reform our system of governance if we are to build a new and better Ireland and I do not believe, despite the rhetoric, that any party in the Dáil is prepared to take the steps that must be taken. They will have to be pushed and this is my contribution to that effort.

There will be those who say this is a book about everyone else being out of step. It isn't. Within the context of illustrating what I think is going wrong I have attempted to introduce as much as possible a third voice or offer checkable evidence. I don't want the message I am delivering to be damaged by the quality of the envelope or the personality of the messenger.

The problem with a book like this is that you need hard, substantiated evidence. Understandably, few people or companies will publicly criticise a Department or a Government they may be clients of and, indeed, may be 'asked' by one or the other to give support on its behalf. When David stunned Goliath, he was very lucky with his aim.

This book is about my political life and experiences but it is also about you, a citizen of Ireland, and the way you live, work and vote and what you think of the way the State operates and how politicians hold it to account, or not. It is you, and every other citizen who votes, who can make the difference, force the changes and build a new Ireland.

This is a small country that has to sell itself in highly competitive world markets. It is essential that every section of our society plays its part. That is why our huge public sector—the State—should be encouraged and led by politicians into becoming renowned internationally for its efficiency, drive and willingness to help—an engine of growth, social security and stability at home, a unique selling point abroad and a provider of exciting, challenging and fulfilling work for its employees.

Currently it is a wet blanket on the fires of aspiration, progress, ambition and social cohesion. It is failing the people who operate it as well as the people and businesses it is there to support.

If you are a teacher, nurse, garda or a frontline worker in a State organisation, I assure you I am not criticising the work you do. This is about what is happening now and what should happen in the future to a system that is so vital to all our lives and to the success of the country. It is about the people who run it and not the people, like you, who hold it together.

There are other engines of growth that badly need to be overhauled, all of them are inextricably linked to Ireland's success or failure: politics, trade unions and our private sector institutions all need to begin giving leadership rather than lip.

It is absolutely essential in this small country that our leaders lead and co-operate with one another as we attempt to regain our feet and their confidence. We do not need turf wars. We need brave decisions.

Every week in my clinics I see the frustration and the growing anger of the old who worked hard in hard times and now have to beg for services; of the State employees who can see the waste and mismanagement but are too afraid of the culture to speak out; of the young now facing emigration; and, perhaps of most concern, of the marginalised to whom the State gave without care or respect and who are now so dependent that they are totally unprepared for the tough times that lie ahead.

I have been a member of Fianna Fáil for 40 years. I know it is a great party, albeit one that has lost its way. I want it now to return to that which made it great, its connections with and involvement in the lives of people and communities throughout our country, from which, under determined leaders, it developed and implemented the policies that put Ireland on the road to success. It should now say it is sorry for having made mistakes and take up the challenge of putting Ireland back on that road, renewing itself and offering the country passionate politics, radical policies and a new brave leadership. We are too great a party to crawl into the next election. We should march into it with our mistakes admitted, a firm resolve to make amends, our backs straight and our heads held high.

To reach a better future, you have to learn from and understand the lessons of the past. With that one can move forward, dream, change, make things better. Above all, I hope this book encourages a debate that is positive about making our lives better. But let us start with the lessons of the past.

One that I will never forget is the Donal Norris case, the extraordinary story of a man, his family, a community and a 9.3 km stretch of the N24 in south County Kilkenny that cost more than double its original budget to complete and would earn notoriety as one of the deadliest stretches of road in the country. You could call it Sanity versus the State.

DONAL NORRIS

One morning in early 2001, I found myself sitting with Donal Norris and his wife Patricia in their kitchen, beside the new N24 Piltown/Fiddown bypass. Those who do not understand what politicians do or have grand ideas about what they should be doing would call my visit to the Norrises 'clientilism'. They would say that I was encouraging Donal Norris to believe that I would get from the State for him that which he could easily get himself. In fact, the Norris case had huge national implications and my involvement with it was to teach me useful lessons I would never forget. What politicians learn in their clinics makes them better legislators.

In fact, Donal Norris had been interacting with the State since 1998, seeking justice but getting nowhere. That is why he had called to my constituency office looking for my help and that is why I was now in his kitchen. Donal had come to me because no one in local or national government would deal with his complaints about the disgraceful treatment he, his family and the community had and were receiving at the hands of Kilkenny County Council, the National Roads Authority, and the Department of the Environment and Local Government throughout the planning, compulsory purchase and construction of the roadway.

I did not know it then but their story of shabby treatment, State bullying and indifference, paltry compensation for flooded fields, a divided farm and damaged buildings was far from unique. In time, hundreds of cases emerged of individuals and communities being bulldozed by the State as the roads programme, funded by billions of euro in EU funds, cut its way through the Irish countryside, shedding millions of euro in waste and shredding the lives of families, with no one apparently accountable for the devastation left in its wake.

The cups and saucers rattled on the dresser in the kitchen as construction vehicles roared past just a few yards away. Distress, sorrow and anger were etched on the faces of this reasonable, decent family as they told me their story. Honest, hardworking citizens of Ireland, they were close to tears as they described their farm being carved up and the time and energy they had used in their frustrating fight with indifferent, arrogant representatives of the State.

It must be understood that Donal Norris was not looking for anything that could be considered unreasonable and I could tell immediately when I first met him that he was no crank. On the contrary, he was a conscientious citizen of this State being railroaded by this State. Donal and the community of Piltown/Fiddown accepted that the building of the bypass was for the public good, which meant some sacrifice on their part, but they did not expect to be totally excluded from the planning process of a project that was to have such an enormous impact on their lives.

There was flooding of land, subsidence to foundations of buildings, vibration damage, the provision of an underpass through which the school bus could not fit and in which animals were injured, a flyover in a location not suited to its purpose and the failure to provide ghost islands or other safety features for the 12 right-hand turns off the road, despite constant appeals by residents and road users. The human cost too was very considerable. There were numerous cases of residents being steamrolled on compensation claims, payments for compulsory purchase orders being inordinately delayed and a general high-handed attitude by officials towards them.

The real difficulty of the local community was that the apparatus of the State excluded them from having any meaningful interaction with it. Common sense proposals were ignored and reasonable suggestions by Donal Norris and others were railroaded. Worse than that, Donal was bullied and threatened by servants of the State, his State, in the most shocking manner merely for trying to vindicate his most basic rights as a citizen. And this was happening all over the country, as was highlighted in a special report by RTÉ's 'Prime Time'.

This was everything I believed might and can happen when individuals are forgotten because of what the State describes as the common good. If, as a member of the national Parliament, I can be shut down by the system when I am only responding to the pleas of a citizen taking on the might of the State, what chance do the marginalised have? The State sets out with goodwill and ambition to care for its people but you need to have a system that is flexible, informal and responsive rather than rule bound and immovable, where the people who operate it become more concerned about sustaining the status quo than serving the public. The State too often demands of people that they observe and keep those rules for the common good that the State and its many arms break without compunction. It is a case of 'Do as I say and not as I do'. And that is a recipe for rebellion.

The essence of my concern is that there has to be a point where the rights of citizens must trump the system's. Like the Great Oz in *The Wizard of Oz*, operated by the little man behind the curtain with the sound and lighting effects, the system begins to believe in itself to a point that it is self-destructive and not fit for purpose. In short, the House cannot continue to always win. We must begin to turn the tables.

The Norris family and I began a journey that morning that is still not finished but has taught us just how high, steep and threatening are the walls that the State can build when it wants to keep its citizens out. I visited Donal during the summer to talk to him about this book and to catch up with him. Twelve years after his family's ordeal began, he is still fighting to get the State to fulfil its side of the bargain. It is something no family should have to go through.

In the course of this book, you will meet the Norrises again, and many others. I hope it will encourage you to take a long look at where we are and what you will now contribute to the effort needed to make a new Republic.

Chapter 1 ᴗ

A FAMILY ON THE CONTINENT

Fire without smoke, Air without fog, Water without mud, Land without bog.

UNKNOWN, CIRCA SEVENTEENTH CENTURY

This verse refers to the smokeless anthracite coal that was mined in nearby Castlecomer and also the limestone paving of Kilkenny City, which prevented mud on the streets, as well as the acknowledged quality of the hinterland.

BEDROCK

The rock that underlies much of Kilkenny county is a powerful symbol of the transformation that time, pressure and effort can bring about. For centuries, Kilkenny has been known as the Marble City, for the polished limestone from which its medieval effigies, pavements and buildings are made. They begin life as a nondescript grey-blue rock, which slow, careful and patient work by human hands turns into a beautiful, valuable commodity.

Living and working with the stone and its many lovely manifestations in buildings and monuments, added to the Norman genes and influences that are to be found around the county, have perhaps given the people of Kilkenny their mark of difference. Certainly independence, determination and drive in work and in sport and a strong spirit of community have always been very evident in my county.

The bedrock of our society and our economy is the people and communities of Ireland. They are made of strong stuff with boundless potential and their quiet, patient work has achieved remarkable results down through the years. That potential has never really been recognised or encouraged by governments and remains relatively unfulfilled because of lack of support.

What is surprising about this is that the politicians who tolerate this lack of engagement down through the decades were and are themselves, by and large, from that bedrock and must surely have realised its value. Certainly Kilkenny politics taught me respect and admiration for those who quietly get things done for their communities. I cannot believe Kilkenny is unique in this. Our Government and administration owes it to communities to support them and, indeed, it depends on their success since they form the foundations on which this State is built.

The McGuinness family has been involved in the communities of Kilkenny and in politics for well over a hundred years. It is something of an achievement in Irish politics to have a completely unbroken record of serving on local authorities since the late 1800s, often with two members. In that time, the family has given Kilkenny 14 mayors, four councillors, two Freemen of the City, a Minister of State and a Vice-president of the European Council. The tradition is continuing with my son, Andrew, who is now a member of the Corporation and Kilkenny County Council.

I continue to refer to Kilkenny Borough Council, as it is now officially known, as the Corporation because of my frustration with the retrograde Local Government Act 2001. The Act substantially reduced the power of public representatives while increasing those of the Executive, pulling power further away from rather than closer to the citizens. And it also attacked the city's status and title.

It was an act of vandalism perpetrated by people who understood the power of the State and knew nothing about the power of community. It was foolish of the Minister, Noel

Dempsey, to bow to their advice and even more foolish if he initiated the process.

My family's roots go deep in St John's parish, which was, and still is, humorously referred to as 'the Continent', because it is across the river from the Castle and the other three parishes of the city—St Mary's, St Patrick's and St Canice's—and therefore regarded as representing otherness or outsider status in the city. The irony is not lost on me. I have my constituency office on O'Loughlin Road in the parish, directly opposite Nowlan Park, the home of Kilkenny hurling. It is the hub of our modern representation in Carlow-Kilkenny, with a relatively technologically advanced system for helping and supporting citizens, communities and businesses.

JACK MAGENNIS

Four generations ago, following the reforms of the UK Local Government Act 1898, my grand-uncle, John Magennis—using the Anglicised version of his name and known to everyone as Jack—was elected to Kilkenny Corporation. A plasterer by trade but a politician by vocation, Jack had a significant talent that flourished during a 40-year career in Kilkenny Corporation. Family history tells of a working man's hero who took no prisoners and was very outspoken. His wife fretted every week about what would be said about him in the Kilkenny papers because of his tendency to confront civic, religious and business figures when he felt it necessary.

Despite that trait—or perhaps because of it—Jack was elected Mayor of Kilkenny six times. When he was first elected Mayor in 1914, Alderman Joseph Purcell, who proposed him for the position, described Jack as 'one of the most faithful men ever sent to the Corporation, and a better Mayor you could not elect'. On taking the chair, Jack issued a call to arms: 'Let us for the sake of Kilkenny forget the past, let us do our best to raise up the city of Kilkenny and let us act together unanimously for the welfare of this old city of ours.' Jack was re-elected Mayor in 1915 and 1916 and went on to serve again in 1928, 1937 and 1938.

A highlight of his political career was when he proposed that his political leader, John Redmond of the Irish Parliamentary Party, be honoured with the freedom of the city at a meeting of the Corporation on 3 April 1916. This was just a fortnight before the Easter Rising that changed everything, including the 'Home Rule Parliament in College Green'.

The Irish Parliamentary Party or Home Rule Party of which Jack was a member was formed in 1882 by Charles Stewart Parnell, the leader of the Nationalist Party, replacing the Home Rule League as the official parliamentary party for the Irish nationalists elected to the House of Commons at Westminster. Pressing for legislative independence for Ireland and land reform, this constitutional movement was instrumental in laying the groundwork for Irish self-government through three Irish Home Rule bills.

By 1917, Sinn Féin had become well-established throughout the country, including Kilkenny. Local newspapers reported that Sinn Féin clubs were formed in Ballyragget, Barna, Graiguenamanagh, Dunamaggin, and a Kilkenny City branch that proved very popular. It was a time of uprising and political confusion and despite the fact that most people in Ireland had a similar goal, the means was always controversial and the cause of many political differences.

In July 1917, after the death of Pat O'Brien, the Irish Party MP for Kilkenny City, a by-election was called to replace him and it was reported that Sinn Féin had decided their candidate would be W.T. Cosgrave. A member of the Irish Volunteers who had served under Eamonn Ceannt in the Easter Rising, Cosgrave was also a Sinn Féin councillor on Dublin Corporation. He had been interned in Frongoch in Wales since the Rising, having had his death sentence commuted to penal servitude for life. By-elections were also called in Roscommon, South Longford and East Clare, the Sinn Féin candidate in the last of which was Eamon de Valera.

Meanwhile, Jack's Irish Party had not yet decided on a candidate while Sinn Féin's popularity was growing at a rapid pace. The local press was very much behind the party and had hailed Cosgrave as 'the man for Kilkenny', despite the fact that he neither lived nor worked in the constituency—a point that I am sure Jack took every opportunity to hammer home. Eventually Jack was selected as the Irish Party candidate for the city and a representative meeting in support of his nomination was held in the Piper's Hall on Maudlin Street, in the heart of St John's parish. It was an emotional occasion that newspaper reports state had attracted a huge turnout of veterans of the national cause, who lived their lives through the struggles and triumphs of the constitutional movement.

In the end, Jack was defeated by Cosgrave in the by-election for Kilkenny North. Local folklore contends that a number of ballot boxes thought to contain large proportions of Jack Magennis's votes were emptied into the River Nore at John's Bridge in order to secure the victory for Cosgrave, but I am sure much the same story was told by the other side. Spin may be a new word, but it is not a modern concept. Typically, this defeat did not prevent Jack from continuing his role as a strong voice on Kilkenny Corporation and he never suffered another electoral setback. Cosgrave, of course, went on to be the first leader of an independent Irish Government.

As Mayor, Jack was frequently responsible for the Borough Court, a minor civil court, where he would sit as judge and pass fines for petty crimes such as 'hurling in a public place' and various alcohol-induced offences, which were disregarded once the defendant took the pledge and paid a small fine. The court cases were reported weekly in the *Kilkenny Journal* and it seems Jack was regarded as a popular judge with a reputation for being reasonable and fair—necessary virtues for a judge and a politician in his home town.

One of the more pleasant tasks mayors enjoyed then as now was presiding over homecoming celebrations at City Hall for

Kilkenny's many All Ireland-winning hurling teams. Jack was a hurling enthusiast and these receptions are recalled as having been among his fondest memories. I suspect that for at least one of them the celebrations began early, resulting in Jack proclaiming world titles for the Kilkenny team, in a particularly purple part of his speech, making 'the first public presentation to... twenty sterling young Irishmen, the All Ireland hurling champions of the world'.

After a long and distinguished career as an independent, Jack was joined on the Corporation in 1950 by his nephew—my father, Michael J. McGuinness—when he was elected as a Fianna Fáil councillor. Considering the body language and facial expressions in the photographs taken at the time, I am not convinced Jack was overly enthusiastic about the rise of a new generation, but he continued as a member of the Corporation, working side by side with my father until his death on 7 November 1953, three years after he had been made a Freeman of the City.

MICHAEL J. McGUINNESS

If Jack Magennis was the groundbreaker in the family, my father, Mick, ploughed, harrowed and made hay on it. Mick was a force of nature and it is difficult even now to avoid being overawed by his character, actions and achievements. I will do my best, but readers will have to forgive me if the long shadow of the man weakens my objectivity somewhat.

Born in 1921, the son of Henry Joss McGuinness, a labourer in Kilkenny Gas Works, and Anne Croake, who worked as a cook and nanny for the Smithwick's brewing family, Mick was reared in a tight-knit community in Maudlin Street, beside the Nore in St John's parish. The memories remained with him all his life. In his seventies he described it as being:

Everything you needed to live fully and die happy. There were pubs and a butcher's shop on one end and the Continent Club and a school at the other. And in between there were five hucksters' shops, a creamery, a bicycle repair shop, a wheel-wright, a stone cutter, a tailor, a dressmaker, a chimney sweep, cot and net fishermen and numerous musicians as well as a castle, a tower, a church, a graveyard, a brass band and the Mortal Sin.

In these more enlightened times, I am sure the Protestant community will share the now thankfully outdated humour that the 'Mortal Sin' was the nickname children of the street gave to the Protestant Kilkenny College, which was situated on the banks of the river behind the back gardens of Maudlin Street. Perhaps the nickname has a modern use now—today the buildings house the offices of Kilkenny County Council!

The Maudlin Street of Mick's childhood, with its rich sense of identity and its deeply rooted sense of community and common purpose, was a seminal influence on his life. It fostered in him a profound social conscience, an understanding of the worth and rewards of community and an empathy with and respect for working people that informed and influenced everything he did as a politician and much of what we believe in as a family today.

He left school at 15 to take a job in Lipton's, a grocery store in High Street, much to his father's disappointment, because he wanted Mick to stay in school 'until his beard reached the floor'. Mick made that all right by attending night school, achieving first place in Ireland in Retail Practice, Commerce and Procedure and, under the guidance of another seminal influence, Father—later Bishop—Peter Birch, he was awarded an honours diploma in Public Administration and Social Science.

Mick was popular with customers of Lipton's, where he was also a trade union official. He created goodwill by helping them make ends meet during the War, which was a step towards building a base from which to launch a political career. He also came into the public eye in 1947 when, along with Kevin and Mick

Shortall and Pierce Clooney of Maudlin Street, he risked his life in a fishing cot saving people in the great flood of 16 March.

He married my mother, Ita Murphy from Threecastles, in 1943. They had 11 children together, nine of whom are still living. I don't think the poor woman had any idea of the rollercoaster ride and the extraordinary journey on which he was going to take her.

He was elected to the Corporation in 1950, becoming its youngest member and joining Jack Magennis, who was the oldest. In 1952, he left Lipton's to run his own grocery shop in O'Loughlin Road, which rapidly became a social hub with Mick in charge of local government and my mother running social welfare; births, marriages and deaths; and posts and telegraphs—we had the only public phone in the locality.

In one way or another, all nine of their children were involved in Mick's political life. It was impossible not to be. The kitchen was regularly full of politicians and local government officials, one of a number of informal forums held in houses and pubs where the affairs of the city were discussed. This collective approach averted problems and achieved consensus between officials and party leaders before formal Council meetings. I did not learn politics at my father's knee—I learned it in our kitchen listening to talk of plans, plots, revolts, disasters and celebrations.

Mick was enormously proud of the traditions and great democratic institutions of Kilkenny. He served on these bodies when they had considerable power and influence and were facing enormous challenges with very little money. He believed not only that all politics is local but that it had to be local and politicians were not just legislators but community leaders with an obligation to lead, take hard decisions and be a strong voice for those they represented.

He once told me that it was the strength of its roots that kept democracy upright and was absolutely convinced that community, where civic responsibility, involvement and pride could best be nurtured and developed, was the key to a fair and caring social order.

That political philosophy was the beacon that guided his political career. Elected because he was popular but popular because he never allowed it to cloud his vision or interfere with decisions, he never hesitated to grasp nettles and make hard choices and he positively enjoyed the responsibilities that leadership imposed.

Under the chairmanship of local Fianna Fáil TD Jim Gibbons, Mick was the secretary of the Kilkenny Castle Restoration Society, which convinced the Butler family to sell Kilkenny Castle to the State for £50, thus laying part of the groundwork for the tourism industry in Kilkenny. He and his friend, Fine Gael TD Kyron Crotty—a formidable pair—were instrumental in bringing the offices of the South Eastern Health Board to Kilkenny, winning out over Waterford in a highly competitive battle. A win brought about, I understand, by much political cajoling and pushing, which they both embellished in the retelling as the years went by. He helped establish O'Loughlin Gaels hurling club with Jim Gibbons's brother Mick, and was a founder member and secretary of the Kilkenny Beer Festival under chairman and PR genius Bill Finnegan. Despite what its detractors said, the festival put Kilkenny on the map and opened the door to Kilkenny Arts Week, the Confederation festivals and the Cat Laughs Comedy festivals by awakening the city to new possibilities.

His political career was always turbulent, often funny and sometimes infuriating. Enormously energetic, independent, difficult to control and impossible to predict, he loved not only the cut and thrust of politics but also its challenges, possibilities and potential. There was a great deal of Richmal Crompton's 'Just William' character in Mick!

The story of the election of Margaret Tynan as Mayor in 1970 is a great example of this. One of my brothers got a call from Mick in Dublin at 6 o'clock one evening asking him to collect councillor Tommy Delaney from Sandymount and bring him down to Kilkenny in time to vote at the mayoral election that night. Now, my father could have called at 3 o'clock, but that wouldn't have suited him—he wanted a mad dash. So Tommy was bundled into a Ford Anglia estate and driven at high speed towards the City Hall in Kilkenny with the certain knowledge that they would miss the opening of the meeting.

In the Council chamber, at 7.30pm, it was all cut and dried. Tommy was absent, which meant there would be a Fine Gael Mayor. Mick had greater knowledge and other ideas. He rose and asked the meeting to consider and recognise the heroism of the Kilkenny Fire Brigade, which the previous night had put out a major fire in Smithwick's store, barely 50 yards from the City Hall. For 20 minutes he pointed hoses at the building, dragged buckets of water up ladders, wielded axes and suffered burns and near asphyxiation on behalf of the fire brigade members. When he sat down, as he expected, the members of the opposition parties, not to be outdone and certain of success in the main business of the night, climbed ladders faster, suffered greater burns and left themselves without a breath. As Mick sat watching the perform-ance he had created, Tommy Delaney burst into the room, the smoke cleared, jaws dropped—and Mick said: 'It's time we got on with the election.' It was a split vote and the name of my father's choice, outgoing Mayor Margaret Tynan, then chair of Kilkenny Chamber of Commerce, was drawn from the hat. My father laughed for weeks.

During one of his terms as Mayor, when the City Hall was being used as a count centre, Mick refused a request by opposition parties that he leave the Mayor's Room when there was a break in the count, both parties fully realising the trouble and publicity this would bring. The army and the Gardaí were called. They came and went. He stayed. On another occasion, during a fire in the clock tower of the City Hall in 1986, I was with my father as emergency operations were conducted from the Mayor's Room. Over the course of a long night, the fire chief and his men checked in to refresh themselves with sandwiches and a bottle or two of Smithwick's delivered from the brewery. As the fire came under control, I left the two supervisors, my father and the fire chief to it. The fire was eventually put out but my understanding of the matter is that neither of the two supervisors was. Their condition the following morning was, I am informed, a tribute to the depth of their concern for the city and the power of Jameson.

On the other side of the ledger there were times when Mick perhaps went a step too far. I particularly remember the mayoral election of 1987, when Margaret Tynan, now Fine Gael, was the incumbent Mayor. On the day of the election, I was working in the shop on O'Loughlin Road while Mick and Margaret were having a long conversation in our living room, the details of which I would not learn until later that night. We all believed that the election was a foregone conclusion. Independent Fine Gael councillor Tom Crotty was to be the new Mayor, having gone through the usual procedure of obtaining the support of the majority of members. The candidate, certain of election, then goes to inform his or her family with great joy, excitement and honour. He or she would also arrange and pay for a reception for family members, officials and fellow councillors that evening. But this was not going to be one of those elections.

As usual, the leaders of the main parties stood up, beginning with Kyron Crotty of Fine Gael, who heaped praise on his party colleague Margaret Tynan's term as Mayor. I think he was followed by Seamus Pattison of the Labour Party and then it was my father's turn as leader of Fianna Fáil, the party that would be opposing but losing to Tom Crotty. Instead of what was expected, my father told the stunned Council chamber that his fellow members' comments about Margaret Tynan's achievements as Mayor had convinced him that she should be given another term and Fianna Fáil would not be putting forward a candidate.

There was consternation around the table, even among Fianna Fáil members, including me, who knew nothing about what was happening. Fine Gael was in turmoil about supporting Tom Crotty, with whom they had done a deal, against their own Mayor. You could hear a pin drop. Everyone sat dumbfounded, except my father, who now had the happy task of surveying the devastation he had wrought on the other side of the chamber. Nothing was said for what seemed like an age until Margaret Tynan grasped the moment and coolly said: 'Well, if there are no other candidates being proposed, I declare myself elected.' That was it. Margaret Tynan was re-elected. Mick had pulled a stroke that he assured me would have the opposition fighting with one another for years.

Tom Crotty, his family and friends watching from the public gallery, was completely devastated and the reception had to be cancelled. While recognising the political implications of stirring dissent in the opposition and while most of the members enjoyed the political theatre and understood the stroke that was pulled, all of us, on reflection, were uncomfortable with what happened. It was a political step too far—unkind and unnecessary. But there was two of them in it: Mick and Margaret Tynan.

In fairness, Mick took his own political setbacks on the chin and never complained. My father was unsuccessful in two Seanad elections by the narrowest of margins. In 1973, he missed a seat by only half a vote and in 1977 he missed out by only one-quarter of a vote. He was also beaten in the Dáil election in 1961, having been added to the ticket by Sean Lemass. His fortunes were not improved by his decision to have a row with the Irish Farmers' Association over his assertion that rates should be paid by the cattle mart since it was located inside the city boundary. This was not a particularly wise choice for a candidate in a rural constituency, but that was Mick.

He served on the Council of Europe and was for a term Vice-president. He served on and was chairman of both the Municipal Authorities of Ireland and the South Eastern Health Board. He also served on the National Health Advisory Council and represented the Irish Heart Foundation in the south-east region for many years.

Having spent nearly 50 years in local government, he was the longest serving public representative in Ireland by the time he retired. He had been Mayor of Kilkenny seven times and when he died in 2007 he was a Freeman of Kilkenny.

NEXT GENERATION

By 1955, when I was born, Mick was running the family, the shop and anything else he could get involved in. I grew up boning bacon, selling ice cream and listening to political thunder and lightning. No need to tell which I enjoyed most.

By the time I left school after my Leaving Cert. in 1972, I had a pretty good grounding in hard work in the shop and in politics. A local grocery store is a difficult place to make a living and I had been putting up posters and distributing leaflets long before I joined a Fianna Fáil cumann at 16.

I spent a number of years as a water inspector for Kilkenny Corporation—and, yes, I am sure my father's influence helped, but that was obvious to everyone—before leaving to work full time for Fianna Fáil and in the shop and in a transport and ware-housing company that I started, now run by my son, M.J., who kindly left the bank loans with me.

If the grocery trade is difficult, transport is even worse, with its high costs and low margins. Both gave a paltry return for the effort. But at least you learn that hard work doesn't kill and effort sometimes isn't enough. I don't regret either experience: being born with a shovel you can use in your hand is better than a silver spoon in your mouth.

It amuses me to be described as a businessman as if I were a Bill Gates figure. I am not. I am a politician and a social democrat with sufficient experience of business to know how hard it is to start and run one successfully, and who has an ability to organise and earn a living.

My progress in politics was along the hard road: working my way through all levels of the Fianna Fáil organisation to

16 years as a member of the National Executive and long terms as a member of the Corporation and Kilkenny County Council.

The political world and its ways that Jack and Mick knew was dying when I came into politics. Anyway, I am more of a party and organisation man than they were, although I share some of their beliefs and attitudes. I lost badly in Dáil elections before I became a TD in 1997 and retained the trust of the people of Carlow-Kilkenny in the elections of 2002 and 2007, in the latter of which I headed the poll for the first time.

Politics is an important part of my life. Like my father, I am excited by its challenges and possibilities and its potential to make all our lives better. Lucky and privileged to be fulfilled by what I do, I work hard at it and get enormous satisfaction from it. But it carries great responsibilities and the greatest of these is to stand up for what you believe in, because that is one of the reasons politicians are sent to the Dáil in the first place.

I fully realise that the people and my political colleagues have to be persuaded and must be listened to and sometimes you may have to back down, but if you have a case you must make it and take comfort from George Bernard Shaw's comment that 'all great truths begin as blasphemies'.

Mind you, there was a man crying in the wilderness once who lost his head believing that!

Chapter 2 ∿

CITY, CORPORATION, COMMUNITY

A city of encouragement to the peaceable and quiet, of dread and terror to the evilly disposed, and of support for the good.
CHARTER OF 1687 GRANTED TO KILKENNY BY KING JAMES II RE-ESTABLISHING CITY STATUS FIRST GRANTED IN 1609

THE CITY

Kilkenny City has a record of unbroken municipal government that dates back to 1231 and, with the exception of Dublin, possesses Ireland's oldest continuous set of public records, which are still preserved in City Hall. The wonderful *Treasures of Kilkenny* by John Bradley, with photographs by Tom Brett, lovingly reproduces these records and adds careful context. As Bradley writes: 'Far from being records of royal patronage or external domination, Kilkenny's civic documents are part of the story of the slow and interrupted development of democracy as the current political system of modern Europe.'

Kilkenny's claim to city status, of which more later in the book, is based on the royal charter of 1609 granted by King James I, which establishes that '...citizens of the said city, incorporated in form hereafter in these presents mentioned or specified, and their successors shall withal forever by virtue of these presents, be one new body corporate and politic in deed, fact and name, by the name of Mayor and Citizens of the City of Kilkenny'. The principle that democracy starts with the people influences my work far more than party politics.

It is a lasting credit to its architects that the distinctive Tholsel building that contains City Hall on High Street in Kilkenny reflects this democratic instinct. It was built as a toll house by Alderman William Colles in 1761 in an unusual Italianate style with an arcade that covers a piazza at street level, acting to this day as a market-place where people meet, trade, play music and socialise under the benevolent protection of the City fathers—or at least out of the rain. The copper-clad octagonal clock tower provides the regulation of time to everyone in the city, reinforced by the peals of its bells marking every 15 minutes with the familiar Big Ben-style chimes.

The Tholsel has been the City Hall for about 180 years, con-taining the Council chamber of Kilkenny Corporation and the office of the Mayor of Kilkenny. The Mayor, four aldermen and seven councillors, with the insignia of the sword and mace and their uniformed bearers, embody the traditions, history and pride of the citizens.

Networks of communities, sporting organisations, the parishes, Chamber of Commerce, voluntary charitable groups and others radiate out from and interact with the Corporation that, at best, helps to provide a stable centre to all this work, reinforced by pageantry and practical support that adds weight to their activities and binds the entire community together.

THE CORPORATION
The Corporation that my father, particularly, and I knew prior to 2001 was largely made up of people used to wielding power: the older members, from an era before mass media and travel had changed people's views and perceptions, were big characters, significant community leaders and decision makers with a vast knowledge of the system and the city.

At the centre was a number of political families with a wealth of experience between them who had held seats for generations:

Kyron Crotty, a Fine Gael TD, had followed his father Paddy, also a TD, and would be followed by his son, Pat, into the Corporation. Seamus Pattison, TD and later Ceann Comhairle, had followed his father James, also a TD. I had followed Jack and Mick and my son Andrew now continues the line.

I do not understand the negative case the media often makes for political dynasties. It is accepted that sons and daughters follow their parents into professions and it is entirely understandable that they choose a familiar path. Dynasties can go wrong but in the case of the men I served with and in my case they imposed standards and responsibilities, which cannot be ignored or avoided, that we accepted and respected. Of course, the Corporation wasn't just about these families or newer ones like Senator Mick Lanigan and his son. Rather than name all of them, I will not name any, but there were many members down through the years who made substantial contributions and none ever gave less than their best for the city.

Apart from its work, the Corporation was also a testing ground for aspiring politicians, who were faced with taking on TDs and long-serving and experienced members. Little quarter was given and hard lessons were learned. Some people cut their teeth while others lost them, but looking back it was an introduction to political realities that was priceless and is now lost. The removal of the dual mandate saw to that.

Members of the Corporation promoted the rights and entitlements of the people and, at that time, although they had the power to hold officials to account, it was rarely used because, while there was a healthy tension between them, there was also a great deal of co-operation and respect. Officials and politicians, with little money, managed the affairs of the city and, in those years, were remarkably good at delivering and improving public services.

All Corporation meetings were attended by the Town Clerk, who was responsible for managing the city, the City Engineer and the County Manager. They were involved in the debates and the decision making in a manner that mixed political priorities with public service, producing results that spread responsibility between politicians and officials and, while there was a rule book, generally it took second place to common sense and flexibility.

The staff in both the Corporation and the County Council, I think, enjoyed the cut and thrust of local politics. They could see the decision-making process from the arguments of either side through to the consensus that would be achieved and the final vote. They could see the policy developing, which they then implemented with action on houses, roads and sanitation, etc. The Town Clerk, City Engineer and County Manager were involved with members at Corporation meetings, which helped encourage debate, interaction and practical problem-solving. Regrettably, that approach has been largely replaced with one of waving rule books and issuing edicts.

Civic institutions like the Corporation are important because that is where power and people meet in small but meaningful ways. The arguments against it are elitist or economic. The first brings eating bread or cake to mind. Indeed, the French now take great care to involve people in the politics surrounding the decisions affecting their lives and leave a lot of them in the hands of the mayors whom you find in every village in that country. I'm sure there is some corruption and graft but it does not usually go unnoticed, ignored or undealt with in the community and it is, in any case, a small price to pay for keeping tumbrels off the streets.

There is more weight in the economic argument, but I think that should revolve around centralising administrative functions like planning, with perhaps one office dealing with Leinster apart from Dublin, but with adjustments both up and down. I would leave county managers and councils and begin to encourage counties to stand on their own feet across a range of services. If they can do it more cost-effectively for themselves than that which the State expensively supplies, and they surely will, let them get on with it.

Of course, what I am saying is general and therefore easily said and easily challenged but my experience tells me that the people would embrace it and the results could be positively surprising. It is a way of achieving again that working balance between the citizen, politicians and officials that I witnessed. Perhaps the biggest obstacle to its progress would be State resistance. But the process is starting and I don't think the State can stop it.

The following is from an article in the *Times* newspaper from 17 July 2010:

> The Prime Minister, David Cameron, is expected to visit a number of pilot projects where local councils give money to grass-roots organisations, charities and social enterprises to run local services.

Cameron's Big Society idea reflects much of what I believe in and it will be interesting to watch its progress.

Local councillors should embrace this idea and stand up now by demanding change and beginning to debate and investigate how best to proceed. They should not be afraid to think big. Of course, there will be difficulties, but at least there is the comfort that waste, inefficiency and graft is easier to see and prevent on the streets of Kilkenny, for example, than it is within the temples of control in Dublin.

While the senior members had worked with at least three town clerks and county engineers, for most of my time on the Corporation, Donal O'Brien, the Town Clerk who took over from Peter Farrelly, occupied that position. That was true also of Paddy Donnelly, the County Manager. Very different people, they are still to me great examples of what officials can do when they have the confidence to step away from caution in the interest of progress and humanity.

Donal was a thespian and a leading light of the Watergate Theatre's annual pantomime. You were never quite sure if you were dealing with the actor or the official or if what you were doing was going to provide material for the Christmas show. He had an intimate knowledge of the city and its people. A Kilkenny man, an actor and a clever official had come together in a Town Clerk who ran the City Hall firmly and who could be, in turn, grumpy, amusingly cynical and very funny. At Corporation meetings he frequently wore a world-weary, detached expression, from behind which he would listen to some passionate and probably self-serving appeal, knowing full well what the motives for it were. He would then, with relish, gently but firmly place obstacles in front of the galloping member that put manners on him without bringing him down. He never allowed surprise to cross his face but, when pressed, his putdowns could make it cross yours. Donal was an able and efficient official with a comprehensive understanding of local government. He seldom put a foot wrong and if he stepped on a politician's toe it wasn't an accident. But he would go the extra mile with you if you made a good case.

On the other hand, Paddy had everyone running extra miles. Charming and urbane, he was a positive, enabling rather than negative, version of Sir Humphrey in 'Yes, Minister'. From the 1960s, he provided guidance, assistance and energy to all sections of Kilkenny society and established relationships with politicians that brought long-lasting benefits to Kilkenny. He shaped my view of how officials and politicians should interact for the greater good of the community. Donnelly was an official who understood and liked politicians and knew what co-operation between the two could achieve. A former parliamentary secretary to Neil Blaney, then Fianna Fáil and, later, Independent Fianna Fáil TD from Donegal North East, he had a great understanding of national and local administration and politics. He knew how to get things done.

Better still, Paddy knew what he wanted to do and he brought politicians with him or facilitated them when he believed in what they wanted to do. He was capable of anticipating and defusing conflicts before they developed and achieving inter-party co-operation for major projects and initiatives, working and negotiating with party leaders within the Corporation, local TDS and Government departments as the *de facto* economic development officer for the city and county. Paddy could effortlessly blunt the point of the sharpest pin and it was a pleasure to work with him.

He remains today, in my mind, the best example I can call on to demonstrate what can be achieved when politicians work with good, motivated civil servants, unimpeded by red tape but constrained by common sense and duty. During the transition between the pre- and post-2001 Local Government Act, he was willing to allow the public representatives to continue to be centre stage and make the decisions to a large extent. He was passionate about new ideas and projects and his skills as a negotiator and conciliator nipped early problems in the bud and fostered consensus. He was in many respects Kilkenny's very own T.K. Whitaker.

My position today about the public service is much misunderstood. I know and respect the work the people in it can and do carry out and it is hugely important to the success of our country. Maybe Paddy Donnelly and his team spoiled me, because they showed me how high the bar could be set. What happened to that culture, that can-do spirit? You can't think big if you are producing and being guided by small print. Between 1960 and now, our public service has largely turned inwards, leaving politicians and the public and, maybe, democracy at the gate, appearing now to believe that its job is to impose order rather than lead and guide change. What happened to the Paddy Donnelly outlook?

I think the Local Government Act 2001, a monument to the bureaucratic desire to control, marked the end of a public service capable of producing powerful vocational public servants like

Donnelly and O'Brien and the end of a democratic local system influential enough to attract powerful politicians to interact with them. I believe this causes huge problems for the management of local authorities today. The tension between officials and politicians has gone. A whole new set of rules and regulations governing city and county were handed down. Public servants now have a rule book in one hand and enforcement powers in the other and little or no tolerance of dissent. Furthermore, they no longer have to deal with strong political figures. TDS have seen their experience sidelined. They are no longer there to challenge or show less experienced politicians how to challenge and set standards for them. Elected politicians now rubberstamp local authority decisions because they can't stop them being implemented.

There is now no need for a Donal O'Brien to create obstacles and steer a debate or a Paddy Donnelly to encourage, support and create. You just open the rule book. The whole notion of public representatives making decisions at local level has gone out the window, and with it, democracy.

Essentially, the argument for all this is that running a country is much too serious to leave in the hands of a venal and self-serving lot like politicians. And in times when the profession was being damaged by a few scoundrels, most politicians kept their heads down and swallowed the line that virtually any public service should be taken 'beyond political influence'. Instead of being turkeys voting for an early Christmas, they should stand up and say: 'Yes, there are problems, but we are worth having. We represent the people and bring a great deal of experience and common sense to the table. We do difficult, necessary and mean-ingful work and, being all too human ourselves, we introduce humanity to a process that can quickly squeeze it out.' Venality and self-service aren't just confined to politicians, they are human failings found everywhere, as we now know to our cost.

In the last four years, this country began to learn that 'beyond political influence' means being largely beyond public scrutiny.

Maybe it would be a lot better and easier to empower and occasionally put manners on politicians than it is to pay the price and suffer the abuse that arises when a system or culture begins to be a law unto itself—banks, bishops and FÁS all spring to mind. Ireland could do with a debate about what lesser evils it is prepared to tolerate for the greater good. Hopefully, the result would be smaller rule books, greater humanity and much more personal responsibility and accountability.

Let me drive that point home.

I know a great deal about planning regulations. People come to me with their plans before they lodge them to check that they are on the right track, sometimes because they are not getting help from officials. A few years ago a man with a plan turned up at my door: a small builder who had permission to knock an old mill and build six or seven houses. However, he had fallen in love with the mill and he now wanted to carry out a sensitive conversion and he proposed to reduce the number of houses. It sounded good to me. What was the problem?

The planners had told him that if he retained the mill he would have to have flora and fauna and archaeological investigations done, which would be hugely expensive. He said to them in various rising tones that he had permission to knock the mill. 'Ah yes, but if he kept it, the rule book said, bats, otters, etc. etc. would be affected. Sorry.'

I told him I thought this was crazy, but maybe if I went with him to the planning office I might be able to break the impasse as clearly a little bit of flexibility was needed. We arranged a meeting.

At the meeting, we encountered rats and bats, butterflies and bees and huge expense, but no flexibility. The rule book said under paragraph X, subsection Y, etc. etc.—'black and white as you can see'.

'But he has permission to knock the mill on top of all those bats, bees, butterflies, etc. etc. without any investigation being done,' I said, getting heated and animatedly moving my hands to demonstrate a flattened building, surrounded by dead flora and fauna and the smell of honey and bat droppings. But the rule book spoke above the din and the smell and I gave up. Before I left, I turned to the official and said: 'This is ridiculous. You haven't heard the end of it.'

The following day I got a call telling me that a charge of bullying and harassment might be taken against me. Another rule book had spoken.

CITY STATUS

Although the progressive centralisation of government in Ireland had been leading to a gradual lessening of the importance of local authorities like Kilkenny Corporation from the abolition of domestic rates in 1977 and throughout the 1980s and 1990s, it was the Local Government Act of 2001, initiated by the then Minister for the Environment and Local Government, Noel Dempsey, that was to signal a major attack on the status of Kilkenny and was an attempt to remove ancient titles and traditions—Kilkenny's historic hallmarks.

The bill was the most fundamental reorganisation of local government legislation since the Westminster Parliament's 1898 Local Government (Ireland) Act and, while it introduced a number of necessary reforms, it contained two specific aspects that for me undermined any good it might do. They related to the removal of the dual mandate, whereby TDs and senators as national politicians would no longer be able to serve as members of local authorities, and the removal of Kilkenny's city status by relegation to a Town Council. With more than 20 years as an intensely proud Corporation member, Alderman and Mayor of Kilkenny, I was set on a collision course with the Minister.

In June 2000, I wrote an open letter to Noel Dempsey, reported widely in the press, which included the following:

There is real anger in Kilkenny among politicians of all parties and among the general public less perhaps because of what the Bill states so badly than by your attitude to the small changes we are demanding. The people who drafted the Bill made a spectacular miscalculation and you have compounded it by not comprehending how important a part tradition and heritage play in the lives of the citizens in this proud, ancient city.

Indeed, in their disregard for history, your officials have put themselves in the same league and have followed the example of two other spectacularly insensitive individuals, both of whom revoked our charter: Cromwell and William of Orange. Not good company, Minister.

We want the fact that we are a city by charter, positively enshrined in the Bill and eventually in the Act. We want our corporation, councillors and aldermen. We want our genuine love for this city and its traditions recognised and respected.

Noel Dempsey made some concessions during amendments to the bill, which came before the Dáil in the summer of 2001, but they were not enough and I made my position clear in the House on 13 June 2001:

The Bill is a Pandora's box which, now that it is open, has allowed a number of issues to escape which many of us want to tease out, tackle and understand more to bring forward legislation which deals with them in a much better way.

We are very proud of the rich heritage and culture which exists there and I consider the trappings of local government, be it the robes or name of Alderman, to be part of our history and heritage. We are proud that we have been a corporation for so long and a city since 1609. We are anxious to retain that structure and I ask that the appropriate amendments be made available as soon as possible so that we can relax in the knowledge that the city status is protected in the Bill.

To remove Members of the Oireachtas from the local government system would weaken it further and would break a unique connection established through generations of politicians between local government and Members of the Oireachtas. It would also kill off the platform of information on many issues confronting the country which we end up airing in this Chamber. As bad as local government might be and as much as it needs reform, this House needs a great deal of reform to make it much more meaningful to the lives of ordinary people.

The bill passed, with Kilkenny retaining the title of Borough Council only, rather than Corporation, but with no greater powers than a Town Council under the legislation. The charters, tradition and practice could continue to be used but only for ceremonial purposes. Symbolically, it was a blow to the status of the city and its citizens but it did not undermine the sense of place and pride that had grown over the centuries. Neither Minister nor rule book can take that away.

COMMUNITY

One of the most outstanding leaders of our community was a man who profoundly influenced my approach to public life, the late Bishop of Ossory, Dr Peter Birch. There are few individuals in the past hundred years who have had such an impact on the social, cultural and economic life of Kilkenny. I was to have the honour of working with him as the youngest member of one of his groundbreaking diocesan committees.

Born into a farming family in Jenkinstown in 1911, Peter Birch was educated at St Kieran's College, Kilkenny. In 1935 he was involved with the Congress of the Catholic Truth Society of Ireland, hosted in Kilkenny, with a theme of 'Social Problems in Ireland'. It was to be a pivotal moment that opened Peter's eyes to the inequities in Irish life and the ways in which they could be redressed.

He had an open and questioning mind, which made him something of a radical. When he established Ossory Social Services together with two Sisters of Charity—Sisters Campion and Stanislaus Kennedy—the group drew on the best modern thinking and techniques on social work at the time. It remains a superb template for how voluntary community groups can co-operate with national and local government and administration for the benefit of the marginalised.

I was politically active and PRO of the Comhairle Dáil Cheantair (the National Executive of Fianna Fáil) in 1977, getting out positive information to the newspapers to promote Fianna Fáil's reputation. There was a new interest and enthusiasm among a large number of young people who were becoming involved in politics and community activism at the time. I guess it was because of my youth and the profile I had in the community at that stage that I was invited to become a member of Dr Birch's diocesan committee.

I began working with Dr Peter Birch, Monsignor Fitzgerald and Sister Stan, helping the group to connect with other young people and encouraging them to become engaged with their community. We also reached out to business leaders to involve them in finding solutions to social problems in the city and county. This was real action with tangible results such as meals on wheels and Kilkenny Social Services.

I can clearly remember the fulfilment and enjoyment I got from the sense of society and community we fostered in helping people to help themselves and eliminate some of the barriers to progress that bureaucracy often creates. Our initiatives were local, simple to operate and very cost-effective. People began to be empowered before that term became widely used. The return on any investment made by the State was significant too. It was true then and remains true today that local initiatives guided by trust, common sense and common purpose can save the State a small fortune—empowerment and reduced central control is what the

State should be about. I began to feel strongly that if the energy I was experiencing could be brought to bear on the structures of local and national government and on the engagement of politicians with citizens, we would have a far more inclusive society, offer hope to those living on the fringes and maybe end for ever their marginalisation.

ELECTED

With the local elections looming in 1979, I decided to stand. Once again there were to be two McGuinnesses on the ticket for the Corporation election, as there had been when Jack Magennis and my father were seeking election. My father was prepared to share the vote and possibly sacrifice his title as alderman—being one of the first four elected councillors—if it meant I would get a seat too.

For the purposes of canvassing and to maximise our vote, we divided the city between us. I started on one side of the city in Walkin Street in St Mary's parish, while Mick started on the other side of the city in the Continent of St John's, where I would finish at the end of the campaign on home turf, so to speak. By the time we approached polling day we had more or less canvassed the entire constituency twice. We encouraged families we knew to be supporters to divide their vote: the older people voting for my father and the younger ones voting for me. It was something of a risky strategy, but it paid off and we were both elected, winning two seats from Fianna Fáil's total of five on the Corporation, which was the party's strongest ever position and has not been equalled since.

Local politics in the city throughout the period was very much dominated by a number of strong political families. Voters crossed and still cross party lines to vote 1, 2, 3 for a combination of Crotty (Fine Gael), Pattison (Labour) and McGuinness (Fianna Fáil). I was elected along with Mick because some of the Crotty and Pattison transfers came to us. This strategy worked again in the 1985 local elections, when we were both re-elected to the Corporation. However, the County Council elections were quite different. I failed to be elected to the County Council for the Tullaroan Electoral Area, losing out to Pat Millea, a man who would later turn out to have a central role in my career. My father, who had served on the County Council since the 1950s, lost out by just two votes.

In the 1991 elections, however, we managed the vote sufficiently well that, even though we did not substantially increase the numbers, we were elected to both the Corporation and the County Council.

The Corporation was dominated by the families I mentioned—the Crottys, Pattisons and McGuinnesses—but there were also other big characters who came and went on the Corporation. Some stayed, like Tommy Martin, Tommy Delaney, Mick Lanigan and Margaret Tynan, all serving as mayors in their time, giving distinguished expression to Kilkenny's creative spirit. At Corporation meetings they took the lead in set piece events like the striking of the rate and the annual election of Mayor, which could result in scenes such as that described earlier in the cases of Tom Crotty and Tommy Delaney.

Tommy was a great mentor to me and a great supporter of my father. He was a union official in Smithwick's brewery and the local organiser of the Gaelic League. His home was a hive of political and social activity. He was a great Kilkenny man, and much loved for his fearlessness—there were no half measures with Tommy. He always used both barrels and, incidentally, two languages in the chamber. He was Mayor when he died and that was very fitting.

The annual striking of the rate, which had to be paid by local businesses alone since the abolition of the domestic rate in 1977, always caused trouble. As the lead public official, the County Manager would present the rate to the Corporation members and a discussion would take place about water charges, public lighting, pavements, refuse collection, waste water and sewage. This would lead to a heated debate, fired up by the importance of the people who would be paying the rate, to the city and to the members' political interests—a very good example of public interaction. Invariably a row broke out about how the financial circle could be squared and political gain could be achieved. But ways were always found to get it done in the end.

Many of my early days on the Corporation were spent learning the ropes, understanding procedures and becoming familiar with the personalities of the members, separate from any information Mick might give me with all the axes he was grinding. Obviously there were differences but there were also deeply engrained positions. The Labour Party would talk to us but not conclude a deal with Fianna Fáil because Seamus Pattison did not like us— he might have softened a little about that after Fianna Fáil made him Ceann Comhairle—and Fine Gael wouldn't deal with us either, until I managed to make an agreement with Kyron Crotty in 1996. It was a tough apprenticeship. Mick just stood back and allowed me to learn my own lessons, and even provided some opportunities.

Politically, the Corporation also introduced me to some of the more complex internal machinations of Fianna Fáil throughout the county as distinct from the election of members of the Corporation. In those years it was difficult to get a Fianna Fáil nomination for County Council elections and it was difficult to get elected because of the breakdown of the constituencies. There was the Corporation in Kilkenny with which we were intimately familiar but the County Council involved electoral areas that were not as well known. They required much hard work and different strategies.

During those early years on the Corporation, when I was also secretary of the Comhairle Ceantair (the County Executive of Fianna Fáil) the party purchased a premises in Collier's Lane near the Friary. It was used by TD Liam Aylward to hold his clinics and

I saw how he managed them as a means of building a support base in the city through personal contacts with city clients. I decided that, as a member of the Corporation, I would begin to hold weekly clinics in Collier's Lane to build a base of my own. Through watching Liam, I began to understand the critical importance of Kilkenny City for Dáil candidates. I first put the theory to the test in the general election of February 1982, polling 970 votes. It was a start.

As a member of the Corporation, hoping that I might one day have an opportunity to try for the Dáil, I spent a great deal of time building up support within the Fianna Fáil organisation and within the city. I remember one Corporation meeting where I placed 20 or 30 motions on the agenda calling for repairs to be made to local authority houses whose numbers I supplied. This allowed other members to identify the occupants and some were concerned that they might be losing supporters. The questions raised were genuine but the supplying of the numbers was political mischief.

I use this example deliberately because it raises the question of clientilism, which I am happy to deal with. I am a practising politician in a profession that represents. I was representing people who needed action and a voice. In this I am no different from a solicitor or an accountant. I need votes to stay in a profession I like, they need fee income and we both need clients. Yes, some clients stay loyal because of my actions. But is that not true of the professions also? Maybe it is the glad-handing and forced goodwill you don't like. What about professional individuals and companies networking at sporting and social events and providing their clients with tickets? Or, perhaps, you think politicians are not, well, you know, proper? OK then, you'd better vote for Church leaders, bankers and builders. Humanity is messy. Give me alternatives.

It is not unreasonable to want to succeed in your chosen profession. To do that clients, or voters, are needed. Indeed, in most professions now the fee income you generate is a powerful promotional measure. To what lengths do professionals go to meet that standard?

I am a professional politician. I work to the best of my abilities for people and for the country. As with all professions, after that it is about the standards you have and the lines you draw.

Chapter 3 ～

INSIDE THE PARTY MACHINE

After 1973, Fianna Fáil was a party in turmoil. As members of what many believed was and should be the natural party of Government, they were not accustomed to being in Opposition and it didn't much suit them. The party had lost the election that year to a Fine Gael-Labour coalition, having enjoyed uninterrupted power for the previous 16 years. Ministers had lost the trappings of office, including their chauffeur-driven State cars, and now had to return to their day jobs and the pay of a TD at the time was not as generous as it is today.

The fall-out from the Arms Crisis also continued to cast a long shadow over the organisation. The aftershocks of the crisis continued to drive deeper wedges that would ultimately lead to an acrimonious split and the foundation of the Progressive Democrats by Des O'Malley and others in 1985.

It was during the run up to that disastrous election, in February 1973, a few weeks ahead of my eighteenth birthday, that I took a job as a water inspector for Kilkenny Corporation. The tools of my trade were a key for opening inspection covers and a stick with a timber bulb at the end used for listening to leaks in underground pipes. You could say it was a skill that stood to me when I went on to work in the Public Accounts Committee, although the covers were more difficult to open and the leakage of money we were looking at was more like a flood.

It was actually my aunt Nancy, rather than my father, who

really got me involved in politics. Mick really didn't make any attempt. At the age of 16, after an AGM, I was inducted into the organisation by Nancy and senior members such as Jack Quinn and Dick Burke, the latter a Corporation member.

Nancy was the secretary of the cumann and a very active one at that. She had a tremendously good-humoured approach to city politics and thoroughly enjoyed the social events she helped create around it. By the time my father had discovered I was a member of the cumann, I was already well-established. At that early stage he was not particularly encouraging of my infiltration but he did not object either.

Much later, Nancy, whom I loved dearly, was to be another factor in my rising concern about Brian Cowen. I asked him, as the leader of Fianna Fáil, to write to her family after she died and acknowledge the more than 50 years of service she had given to the organisation. It was a request that Bertie Ahern would have understood and acted on immediately. After all, it would take only a letter. Cowen did nothing, so I wrote to him. He still did nothing. I spoke to him again, still nothing. It was disappointing. I wondered how this man, who could lecture us on the need for loyalty to the party, had so little loyalty or respect for the unpaid party activists, of whom Nancy was just one of many thousands, who kept it alive. Talk is cheap.

Parallel to my being secretary of the cumann, I was elected to the Comhairle Ceantair. This required canvassing and an increasing amount of public speaking. It was a time of great enthusiasm and energy in the party and cumann membership was multiples of what you would find now. There was ruthless competition for positions within the organisation as well as for nominations as a candidate for election.

By the time I became involved, the party in Kilkenny had its version of Verona's Montagues and Capulets, the leaders of which were Bob Aylward and his sons Bobby and Liam, with a base in the strongly republican south of the county, and Jim Gibbons in the north of the county. It was a competitive and aggressive political environment.

Fianna Fáil was a great nationalist movement with exciting charismatic national figures like Brian Lenihan Sr, Charlie Haughey and Dessie O'Malley. At the time, I would have regarded Fine Gael as a party of complacent conservative professionals and one that seemed in that turbulent era to be more sympathetic to Northern Ireland Unionists than the embattled nationalist minority. For a young person, strong republicanism and the faint whiff of cordite around Fianna Fáil made it compelling before you even considered family affiliations.

The appointment of Séamus Brennan as general secretary in 1973 had begun to make a difference in the party and its fortunes were improving around the time I joined. A new youth wing—Ógra Fianna Fáil—was established by Jack Lynch in 1975 at the behest of Brennan to capture a growing interest in politics among the young people of Ireland. I soon found myself in the role of secretary of the Comhairle Ceantair. I was encouraged to contest election to the National Executive and was elected as a member in 1976, a position I held for 16 years, which gave me a cockpit view of the party through the eras of Jack Lynch and Charles Haughey.

Over the years, Jack Lynch has garnered an unfair reputation as having been a somewhat soft and lightweight leader. He was seen as a mild-mannered man who lacked the steel for the cut and thrust of high-level politics and, in that, underestimated. On a political level he was also regarded as having been something of a compromise place-filler following Sean Lemass's early exit from the national stage in 1966. Lynch's elevation to the leadership did avoid what would have been a destructive battle between Charles Haughey and George Colley at the time, but he was no place-filler.

The truth is that he was one of the party's toughest leaders. When he played hurling for Cork it was said he was more than capable of digging the handle of his hurl into an opponent's ribs to soften him up—you don't win six All Ireland medals behaving like an altar boy. When he was forced into it he could be decisive and ruthless. I remember a number of National Executive meetings at which arguments threatened to get out of control and he just came out with all guns blazing and shut the whole thing down. Having listened to a debate that was the complete opposite of the point of view he had just expressed, he would ask: 'Is there any dissenting voice?' There would be a long silence but no dissenting voice. 'Then that's the position of the party,' he'd conclude. It's likely he copied this technique from Sean Lemass, whose approach to Cabinet deliberations was very much more presidential than some of his successors.

I liked Lynch. He was cautious and reflective but he had a common touch. He was also able to separate himself from the party and, while he ruled it with a firm hand, I think he was wary of its tribal instincts, being cerebral rather than emotional.

Séamus Brennan's impressive management of the Mount Street headquarters was a new departure in many ways from the old Fianna Fáil. More than anyone, he was responsible for modernising the party organisation at that time. He worked with party veteran Jack Carroll in Mount Street and began to re-organise all the party's records and institutional knowledge into a modern businesslike format. Brennan was open to dynamic new thinking and new ideas and he was not afraid of change.

I had the great fortune to be employed by the party at head-quarters in 1976, ahead of the anticipated general election in 1977. Work in the office would begin at 6.30 every morning with meetings sometimes chaired by Lynch himself but more likely by Séamus Brennan, who was a dynamo in his role. Fresh, exciting ideas were discussed and there was a palpable sense of energy, enthusiasm and optimism about this revived organisation. Young people with little or no profile then, like Mary Harney, were sent around the country to address cumann meetings and rebuild the organisation through its community, county and constituency branches. We motivated, monitored the reactions on the ground and reported back to headquarters. The party could do with someone like Séamus Brennan today.

The response we got travelling around the country began to convince us that this newfound self-belief, together with the unpopularity of the Coalition Government, meant that Fianna Fáil was ready for an election and ready for government. Despite these grass-roots developments, the parliamentary party believed they had no chance of winning the election. For one, Jim Tully, Fine Gael's Minister for Local Government, had loaded the dice with the ruthless redrawing of constituency boundaries that significantly favoured the Government party. It became known as the Tullymander.

Meanwhile, back in Kilkenny, Liam Aylward was a young candidate and headquarters encouraged us to support him, because we had a chance of winning two seats for the party. There was a surge of support for younger candidates and we wanted to tap into the growing interest that young people generally were taking in politics at the time. This was also reflected in their enthusiasm for initiatives that were being pursued by people like Peter Birch. I gravitated towards Liam Aylward. He was young, had a big and well-organised machine and the party was fully behind him.

The Aylwards had a pillar of support in Kilkenny City, led by Senator Mick Lanigan, and although the imperative was there from the party to return two seats for the constituency, it was also important to the Aylwards to block any upstarts, like the McGuinnesses, from building their own base.

Historically, the McGuinnesses, in general elections, did not side obviously with any Fianna Fáil candidate—it was usually politically advisable not to. However, on this occasion, we supported Liam Aylward, perhaps because of my father's on-off relationship with TD Jim Gibbons. That support did not lessen Liam's subsequent determination to put the brakes on my aspirations. It was a closed shop and that was how he wanted to keep it. I understood his position, but that did not mean that I would not challenge it if I got the chance.

Back at headquarters, an election strategy committee was set up under the chairmanship of Senator Eoin Ryan Sr and Séamus Brennan's minute attention to detail and strict timelines were applied to the tasks to be undertaken as the campaign kicked off. This was a full-scale American-style election campaign the likes of which Ireland had never seen. Advertising agencies were hired to advise. There was high-quality print material and photography. Opinion polling and focus groups were undertaken and media experts were employed to interpret and spin the results. There was even the campaign song: 'Your Kind of Country' sung by Colm C.T. Wilkinson, which we distributed throughout the country in our cars. It was a totally professional campaign with carefully co-ordinated and sequenced speeches, media appearances and policy announcements.

If the fatalistic parliamentary party knew little about the preparations for this blockbuster of an election campaign, they knew nothing about the mysterious manifesto. That said, neither did the primed and ready machine in Mount Street.

The Fianna Fáil manifesto for the 1977 general election was prepared in secret by Martin O'Donoghue and a small number of others. O'Donoghue had been appointed as economics adviser to Jack Lynch at the end of the previous Fianna Fáil Government and held that highly influential role while the party was in Opposition. He was a dry and remote character who knew much about the theory of politics but really he had no feel for how it works on the ground. Work on modern policies was carried out by various specialist committees, unknown to the parliamentary party and certainly kept secret from the Coalition Government.

When the Fianna Fáil manifesto was finally revealed, less than 24 hours after the election date was fixed by Taoiseach Liam Cosgrave, no one was prepared for its extraordinary largesse. Among other treats it called for the abolition of car tax and domestic rates, a £1,000 grant for first-time house buyers and it promised to reduce unemployment to below 100,000. The incumbent Government had squandered the advantage of dictating the timing of the election by being totally unprepared for the Fianna Fáil onslaught. The public and the media bought into the extravagant proposals and there were few dissenting voices.

Charles Haughey did, however, privately express serious concerns about the long and short-term costs of these measures, probably because Lynch was in charge, but no one wanted to spoil the party. It has to be said that later in his career, Haughey was not averse to buying an election with promises himself. In this, he was no different from other party leaders.

We were reporting back to headquarters that candidates and senior members were speaking to huge crowds. Fianna Fáil was riding a wave of popularity. This had more to do with the widespread unpopularity of the Coalition Government of Fine Gael and Labour under Liam Cosgrave and the trust and affection Jack Lynch inspired than it did with the bonanza manifesto. A number of experienced hands told the party leadership that it should row back on the promises. Neil Blaney TD, who knew more than most about politics on the ground, was also saying they were unnecessary.

Martin O'Donohue, Séamus Brennan and the conclave that put together that manifesto were working in isolation at an academic remove from what was happening in the country. They had no real feel for it and no feel for how politics works outside Dublin. Blaney did. He knew the truth of Tip O'Neill's dictum that 'all politics is local'. We centralise our political life at our peril. Politicians need to have a close ear to the ground at all times if they are to truly advocate for those they represent.

During the election, Mick got up to his old tricks again. He used posters in the front windows of the family shop in O'Loughlin Road to advertise 'The Coalition Price of Butter' as well as bread and groceries, which he changed on a regular basis to reinforce the deep dissatisfaction with the price inflation over which Finance Minister Richie Ryan was presiding. That the window was not broken and none of the customers complained about this brazen political messaging was testament to the desire for change that was sweeping the country, although no one had yet defined it. Fine Gael- and Labour-supporting customers may have lost their temper on occasion—much to my father's mischievous delight—but we never lost their custom.

The country was in serious financial difficulty. People had been penalised by the Government through its taxation and fiscal policies for a number of years and, by the time they got to the 1977 election, had made up their minds. Like now, there was a huge sense of disillusionment and despair with the Government and politics in general. That summer, with Fianna Fáil at the height of its powers, I was aboard a runaway election campaign with towering national figures like Brian Lenihan Sr, Charlie Haughey, George Colley, Gerry Collins and Des O'Malley. It was an extraordinarily exciting buzz.

Of course, some of the legacy of that ill-conceived manifesto is with us today. The abolition of domestic rates caused great damage to local government and real local democracy. Since 1977, local government has had to be funded principally from central government and with this central funding came a much greater degree of centralised control, moving democracy further and further away from the citizen. A number of initiatives in recent years have attempted to re-introduce elements of domestic rates on a piecemeal basis but they are politically extremely difficult to pursue, particularly in such challenging economic circumstances. Political corrections, such as new water charges, from which local authorities will have to raise revenue to pay for the treatment and distribution of water supplies, are being considered. It's not a popular position, but the reality is that domestic rates payable to local authorities make local politics serious and connect people in a direct way with their politicians—paying rates demanded an accountability and transparency that is lacking today.

The Americans have a phrase, reflecting one of the causes of their Revolution against British rule, that there should be 'No taxation without representation'. In Ireland, we have at local government level 'representation without taxation'. Democracy must work at its lowest constituent level for it to truly serve the citizen as intended. This is how my father and Jack Magennis before him operated on Kilkenny Corporation and County Council. Local government in Ireland needs to go through a renaissance of sorts. It needs to have powers reinvested in it that have been slowly stripped away over the past 30 years or so. Local political representatives then must be able to hold the Civil Service managers of these authorities to account on behalf of the citizens. And the citizens must hold their political representatives to account for their decisions and their actions.

I continued to serve on the National Executive through Jack Lynch's period as Taoiseach up to his retirement in 1979, when the long-awaited leadership battle between Charlie Haughey and the then Tánaiste George Colley finally took place. Colley had the support of almost the entire Cabinet, who distrusted Haughey as much for his naked ambition as anything else. However, Haughey had the sometimes fanatical support of a majority of the Fianna Fáil backbenchers, who were principally concerned about keeping the seats all too easily won in the 1977 landslide. The race was very close and Haughey won by 44 votes to 38, creating a cleavage in the party that was to remain throughout his leadership and provide the focus for numerous 'heaves' against him.

I was impressed by Charlie Haughey's exceptional political abilities, but there was a part of his personality that overshadowed what he was doing. Ultimately, his desire for power and the trappings of power undermined his effectiveness and perhaps denied the country the greater and more positive impact he could have made. He had immense talent and the ruthlessness all successful leaders must have but his grip on the party was too great and too tight. Dissent was increasingly prohibited and the moral slippage that frequently accompanies sycophancy crept into the soul of the party.

Charles Haughey took a wrong turn at one of life's crossroads for whatever reason. Had he turned the other way, his contribution to this country would have been even greater than it was because he had the brains, the confidence and the personality in abundance.

Haughey's relationship, or rather lack of it, with Fianna Fáil TD Jim Gibbons was key at this point. Gibbons had been Minister for Defence during the Arms Crisis of 1970 when Haughey and others were suspected of arranging to have arms imported and distributed to groups in Northern Ireland where the nationalist and Catholic community had come under attack from Loyalist mobs backed up by the RUC and B-Specials. Jack Lynch sacked Haughey and Neil Blaney from Cabinet and a criminal case was prepared for court. As the responsible Minister, Jim Gibbons was the chief witness for the prosecution and testified in the court case against the defendants, who included Haughey and Blaney as well as an Irish Army intelligence officer, James Kelly; Belfast republican leader, John Kelly; and a Belgian businessman, Albert Luykx. Gibbons's evidence contradicted that of Charlie Haughey yet, because Haughey was acquitted, it was Jim Gibbons who was considered to have not told the truth. I have no comment to make, because the trial was full of smoke and mirrors. But I will say that the Jim Gibbons I knew was an honest man.

Closer to home, my father had a love-hate relationship with Jim Gibbons. Mick was the constituency briar whom you ignored at your peril and Jim, a national politician and Minister, was not that comfortable with grass-roots politics. His was a sophisticated view. In my early days as secretary of the Comhairle Ceantair, I worked closely with him. I remember well the powerful smell of his French Gitanes cigarettes as we travelled in his Peugeot 504 around the bohreens of Carlow and Kilkenny attempting to repel the advance of Liam Aylward's organisation, already dominant in south County Kilkenny. I could see the benefits and necessity of mixing both approaches to politics and that is what I do now. But Jim did find the grass-roots work tiresome.

Sitting with him at the top table during cumann or local meetings was often hilarious. To relieve his boredom, Jim, a gifted cartoonist, would begin sketching someone with a bonnet full of bees while talking to me under his breath. There was nothing unkind about this. Jim was just amusing himself and anyone who ever went to a meeting will know there are people with bees in their bonnets who are never satisfied.

'Now, John,' he would say, 'look at Jack and Molly over there. Their concern is a bend in the road on which no one has died or ever will.'

The pencil would be flying across the page with Jack and Molly getting the full treatment.

'You can't stop them talk, John—the bend is their life, God bless them.'

Jim wasn't blessing them. Molly now had a large wart on her nose and Jim's pencil had turned Jack's ears into cabbages. In the hall, Jack and Molly were rehearsing yet again the dangers the bend represented. No one was listening. Everyone in the room had been around that bend too many times.

On the platform, Jim now had a drip coming from Jack's nose, Molly was developing crossed eyes and his muted commentary was like his cartoon—getting closer and closer to the bone.

It was hilarious and keeping a straight face was almost impossible.

Jim Gibbons was a gentleman and a fine politician. I liked him a lot and I learned a lot from him.

In the late 1970s the local Fianna Fáil organisation invited Jack Lynch and Charlie Haughey to a public function in Kilkenny. In our house there was an old public phone with the A and B buttons, which serviced the whole neighbourhood. One evening the phone rang and my mother answered it. I could hear her saying: '…and I'm Marilyn Monroe.' She called out: 'John, you're wanted on the phone—some eejit calling himself Charlie Haughey.' So I went down and took the phone not knowing what to expect. 'Hello, Charlie Haughey here,' came the familiar voice. 'You invited me to a function along with Mr Lynch,' he said. 'We're busy men. Do you know how many constituencies there are in this country?' I was flustered and couldn't think straight. I said: 'Yes I do.' 'Well, I have to cover all of those,' said Haughey. 'How many?' he asked. I hesitated. I couldn't think of the number off the top of my head. He hung up.

Towards the end of his time as Taoiseach, we eventually did succeed in bringing Haughey to Kilkenny and he drew 1,500 people in the Newpark Hotel at an event to honour the councillor Jack Murphy and my father. That night I saw a man who was adored by ordinary members of the organisation but seemed completely confused by it. Somehow he had lost the connection. His speech was good but it didn't relate to the context of the event and was without conviction.

Sean Lemass had seen Haughey in action and didn't want him in Cabinet at first, despite the fact that he became his son-in-law. Lemass was in complete control of everything in the party that had been handed to him by de Valera. His entire focus and concentration was on revolutionising the economy with T.K. Whitaker and he allowed himself no distractions. Had Haughey applied himself as exclusively as did Lemass, perhaps he might not have avoided hubris and would have achieved a great deal more, but then that was not his personality.

In February 1985 Labour Party Minister for Health Barry Desmond had introduced the Family Planning Bill that was to liberalise the sale of contraceptives. It was a modest enough bill but the conservative elements in Fianna Fáil and the imperatives of Opposition meant that the party was to vote against it. Of course, free votes on such matters of conscience should have been allowed. Des O'Malley refused to vote with the party on the bill and gave a rousing speech in the Dáil in which he said he would 'stand by the Republic'. This just fuelled the deep animosity between himself and Haughey.

I was a member of the National Executive when Des O'Malley was summoned to a party meeting on 26 February. In the L-shaped room in Mount Street a motion was tabled for his expulsion from the party for 'conduct unbecoming'. It was one of those truly electric moments in politics.

I was impressed that O'Malley attended the meeting, because he was under no obligation to do so. I was even more impressed when he began to speak and it became clear why he had attended. He wasn't fighting for himself but for Fianna Fáil. It was an emotional and convincing appeal to the members to do the right thing. An open roll-call vote was taken and members voted 73 to 9 to expel O'Malley from the party. I was one of those who voted in favour of his expulsion. I regret it to this day, because O'Malley was right and Haughey and the party were wrong.

A herd instinct took over that night. Despite O'Malley's powerful speech, most members were too in thrall to the party's strong tribal culture, encouraged by Haughey. They went with the stampede, as did I. O'Malley was a compelling alternative voice in the party and was an impressive parliamentarian. But that did not stop him being ruthlessly expelled. In retrospect, I decided I would never again allow myself to be swept along in this manner. Herds are too easily stampeded and can go over cliffs. It was a defining moment for me.

There is a fundamental question about how one deals with the collective culture that can grow in an organisation like the Fianna Fáil party or any institution. It leads to the belief that the protection of the institution at all costs is the paramount objective and the independence of the individual within the institution is often challenged and degraded. Indeed, for the culture to survive, individualism and exceptionality have to be eliminated. We have seen this to our cost as so many of the pillars of Irish society have begun to crumble, undermined by their own reliance on blind and unquestioning loyalty—the Church, State and semi-State bodies and politics itself, with the professions lowering their standards and generally participating in a slide to the bottom.

I don't think many regulators did a proper job. Auditing and legal firms have a great deal to answer for because had they been rigorous, a lot of what happened could not have happened.

To prevent a reactionary mindset taking over, new ideas, revision, reform and adaptation have to be promoted and welcomed. Preservation of the old order for its own sake is never a positive instinct and is generally destructive of institutions and individuals. Change and reform should not be something that is forced on us only by occasional crises, but rather should be at the heart of how we govern ourselves and run our public services.

Chapter 4 ∿

YES, MAYOR

HISTORY AND TRADITION

The first Mayor of Kilkenny, Thomas Ley, was elected in 1609, although he didn't serve the full term. It's not known exactly why, but he was replaced later that year by John Rothe, a member of the wealthy merchant family that built Rothe House—one of the most outstanding and best-preserved seventeenth-century buildings in the country. Ley was elected on foot of a charter from King James I that year, conferring city status on Kilkenny, a culmination of 300 years of grants and privileges from the first sovereign, Richard Palmer, back in 1282.

There is a deep satisfaction and pride in being a link, however small, in the history and traditions of your own place and that is what I felt when I was elected Mayor of Kilkenny on 1 July 1996, becoming the third generation of the family to have the honour with, between us, 14 terms in the office. I had been a member of the Corporation at that point for 17 years. In my inaugural speech that evening I asked what Jack Magennis, first elected in 1914, would think of the modern Corporation and Kilkenny City and reflected that he might be disappointed. Despite the fact that it represents democracy in the city, the Corporation had lost much authority and has lost more since. As the inheritors of a great tradition as elected representatives of a great and ancient city, I expressed the view that we must find a way of imbuing City Hall and, by extension, the city with the dignity and significance that had been eroded over time. The way to do this, I felt, was by renewing and encouraging self-confidence among the people and politicians of Kilkenny.

The politics behind the election of Mayor could be a fraught and devious business, as in the case of my father's involvement in Tom Crotty's failed bid, which I related earlier. I had learned a great deal in my time on the Corporation and the County Council from 1979 and I really felt that, around 1995, I was properly coming of age politically. This might sound odd, but you must understand there were commanding figures around who dominated local politics.

I had always been wary of the narrow party politics that pervaded our discourse and strongly felt that the time had come for a new style of politics. I felt that a co-operative non-partisan approach that included the citizens of Kilkenny was needed to foster a new sense of energy and enthusiasm, inspired to a large extent by my experience working with Bishop Birch.

AN UNUSUAL DEAL

For many years, the Mayor of Kilkenny had been elected on the basis of some sort of an agreement between the political parties on the Corporation. The Labour Party, under a future Ceann Comhairle, Seamus Pattison TD, would always talk to us in Fianna Fáil but the talks would drift, nothing would happen and they would inevitably end up in partnership with Fine Gael—Labour would never vote for a Fianna Fáil Mayor. After the local elections in 1994, I set about exploring a detailed partnership agreement with Kyron Crotty, the leader of the Fine Gael group and a close colleague of my father's.

It was very unusual for anyone from Fianna Fáil to approach Fine Gael with a view to doing a deal on the mayoralty but, much to my surprise, I found the door open. It was also my first time to negotiate any kind of an explicitly political arrangement like this. Usually my father or another senior party figure would do the deal making. I had always found Kyron Crotty easy to negotiate with, hard but fair, and I was able to identify with him because he was also in business. Over a period of time I worked out an agreement with him: Fianna Fáil and Fine Gael would come together to elect agreed mayors on a rotating basis.

Crotty was enthusiastic about my proposal, because it called for the appointment of committees within the Corporation, whose membership would be divided among the political parties, giving them the strength of cross-party co-operation and support. The principle of these committees derived from the diocesan committees established by Bishop Birch on which I had served. I could see a very strong case for setting aside party politics, as had my father and Kyron Crotty and others for many years, on particular issues, and establishing a non-partisan alliance to solve the big problems of the community and drive economic and social development.

Won over by the positive and constructive nature of what was on offer, Kyron Crotty agreed to the deal and we finally signed the document that set it out in detail. It was totally against the expectations of the time and even my father was sceptical that a deal could be done. I remember well that when I brought the document back and showed it to him in O'Loughlin Road, he pointed out that Crotty had signed his first name as 'Kyron', about which my father remarked: 'You see, he wouldn't even sign his name right for you so he'll hardly vote for you.' Crotty's Christian name is, in fact, spelled 'Kyron' even though the common usage of it was 'Kieran'.

Signatures were a sore point with Mick, who some years before had negotiated a deal, not with Fine Gael, regarding the mayoralty. When it came to his turn, it was demonstrated to him by one of the supposed signatories to the deal that his signature had been supplied by someone else and that the other signatory was dead. Mick believed it was all deliberate. He wasn't elected Mayor that year and he was sore about it for months.

As I knew would be the case, the deal with Kyron Crotty was followed through to the letter. I never doubted Crotty's integrity or his ability to deliver the Fine Gael side of the bargain. It was a significant moment in my political career and in many ways marked my political independence from my father.

ELECTED

The mayoral election was held on 1 July 1996. My family was in the public gallery, my father in the chamber. I felt reasonably sure he would vote for me! As the vote was called, there was momentary anxiety as I thought about what happened to Tom Crotty. Who knew what plots had been hatched? The outgoing Mayor, Kyron Crotty, called for the nominations for candidates for the position of Mayor. I was proposed along with others and the vote was taken. Fine Gael kept its bargain and I was elected. Kyron Crotty then declared me the Mayor of Kilkenny and he placed the chain of office around my shoulders. It was an emotional moment.

Politicians are largely unsentimental and I am no different. But this was a special honour being bestowed on me by my own in a chamber that had seen a number of family successes and failures for over a century. I felt very proud. That is what tradition does, it slips respect for something bigger and better into your soul. In my inaugural speech that night I again returned to the importance of community and the need for politicians to stand up. This encapsulated my desire to try to make a new politics work and set the bar higher for the city, but it also reflected my broader critical thoughts on how politicians and officials interact in government, both locally and nationally, and isn't much different to what I am saying now, 15 years later.

Politicians are inclined not unnaturally towards a school of thought which says: 'There goes the crowd, I am the leader, I must follow'. As a result we are becoming nothing more than a shield and a mask which an unelected bureaucracy uses to deflect criticism and problems while it quietly and comfortably gets on with the business of running the country. We now spend more time looking for answers than we do making decisions, the whole process is subverting democracy. We were elected to represent the citizens of Kilkenny and they are expected to do just that—from the front. If we are prevented from doing our work properly, it is our duty to stand and give challenge. We were not elected to live on the crumbs of comfort and information which fall from the bureaucratic table.

I called for a reappraisal of the way we treat visitors to the city and county, emphasising that they should be coming to a city that reflected our hopes and ambitions, rather than a spend opportunity reflecting a desire to cash in. I proposed the development of a co-ordinated tourism policy and a Millennium committee to encourage people to 'See 2000 in Kilkenny'. I said I was going to appoint a number of committees, including an industrial development group, a film action group and an information age group as well as a group to work towards the establishment of a university campus in Kilkenny. Finally, I underlined the alienation of the unemployed dependent on social welfare handouts and pointed out that money was no substitute for care.

A NEW BROOM

The weekend after I was elected I turned my attention to the Mayor's office. A small room off the Council chamber, it had all the charm and atmosphere of a police station holding cell, nondescript furniture and objects adding to the air of fatigue and irrelevance. It would not do. Over the weekend I took the contents into the corridor and installed furniture and paintings that gave the room a lift and made it a place that would suggest to visitors that the city was proud and serious about the Mayor and the office. First impressions and self-confidence are important.

Town Clerk Donal O'Brien, as usual, betrayed no concern or surprise when he entered the room the following Monday morning, even though he had to step around the furniture in the hall. I was sitting behind the desk going through messages of congratulations. He complimented me on the changes and we enjoyed a little polite conversation before he made to leave. 'Donal,' I said, 'I can only make local calls on this phone.' 'That's the way it's always been,' said Donal, taking the line of precedent so beloved of officials. 'Not any more,' I said. 'I'm the Mayor and I'm entitled to have the same office facilities you have.' Donal was not prepared to concede on the phone, a secretary, a computer, office equipment or the parking space I wanted—defending precedent was better than creating it. I could see that he wasn't concerned. Now that he had placed all of his obstacles in position, he would see how well I jumped them before taking further action. Having worked with my father when he was Mayor, maybe he wanted to establish if the apple had fallen far from the tree.

But I was determined. It wasn't about me. It was about the position of Mayor and my pledge that I would be a proactive and vigorous Mayor. To do that I needed the basic tools. Furthermore, I believe firmly in the primacy of the elected representatives of the people over the paid servants of the people. I was then and am now absolutely willing to accept the responsibility that this placed on my shoulders. I don't require officials to take my decisions for me but I do require their co-operation, considered advice and respect for any public office I hold.

In Donal's case I would get all of that but I understood his concern about precedent so I rang his superior, Paddy Donnelly, the County Manager. He had heard my inaugural speech and I am sure he was expecting, maybe even looking forward to, an unusual mayoral term. He listened to me and asked me what I was going to do. 'I'm going to do everything a Mayor should do,' I said. 'I'm going to make a difference.' He didn't hesitate. He gave me all I had asked for and his approval. And he and Donal O'Brien gave me their wholehearted support throughout my year as a full-time Mayor.

I thought the Council chamber needed a change and I reconfigured the Clive Nunn-designed furniture so that the members of the Corporation faced the public rather than had their backs to them. We asked the staff to hang paintings by Tony O'Malley, as well as work given by Elizabeth Cope, including a painting by her of my father's beloved Maudlin Street. I also commissioned Michael Jackson, the potter, to make bowls, on the lid of which was the arms of the City of Kilkenny, to be given to visiting dignitaries. Incidentally, Brian Cowen was presented with one in the chamber when he launched my general election campaign in 1997. I wonder if he still has it on his dressing table?

Once we had made the Thosel fit for the purpose of a dynamic mayoralty, I began to open up the building and the Mayor's Parlour to community groups and individuals who wanted to be involved in this new approach to local government. I invited dozens of such groups in to meet with me and the officials and assured them that we were on their side and would do everything we could to help them help themselves. The goodwill generated by this process was invaluable. My instinct for engaging in these meetings was not in any way contrived but derived directly from the approach I had seen taken by Bishop Birch, Sister Stan and others in their work with the diocesan committee and dozens of other outreach groups in which I played a small part as a young man.

I was running a business, which had its own needs, and I had a young family but I was determined to make this year in office really count. I had reached a tipping point in my political career and I was not going to allow myself to be diverted from the plan I had agreed with Kyron Crotty on behalf of the citizens of Kilkenny. I worked long hours every day of the week at City Hall but there was a great sense of achievement and much satisfaction with the co-operation I was receiving and the excitement and energy that was being generated to encourage me and drive me on.

MAYOR'S ACTION GROUPS

One of the main features of the deal I had done with Kyron Crotty, referred to in my inaugural speech, was the creation of various committees of the Corporation that were partly inspired by those diocesan committees and Ossory Social Services. I announced the formation of the action groups at a meeting of the Corporation in the summer of 1996. In my speech I underlined the fact that the vast majority of the politicians who represent the public and officials who serve the public are honest and hard-working but that the system had its weaknesses, again a position I have not moved away from.

In my speech I said:

Democracy in action can be slow, unwieldy and inefficient but democracy is about representing the people whatever the cost. There are now enough bodies in our democratic system to fill Glasnevin and enough boards to build the coffins for them, while at the same time local government is being sidelined and along with it local pride, self-respect and social cohesion.

The working population of Kilkenny is no greater than the workforce of a small multi-national. We need to get our act together, we need to begin to manage our affairs in a business-like, cost-conscious, efficient manner. We need more risk-takers and decision makers from businesses to be involved in the marketing of Kilkenny and they should be encouraged and welcomed by politicians and officials alike. They have a significant part to play.

On the other hand, business people must understand that the skills politicians and officials bring to the decision making process are important too. Prudence, caution and deliberation have their place and I have too much respect for the work done by politicians and officials to suggest otherwise. I am simply pointing out that the pendulum may have swung too far and the balanced introduction of method, attitudes and practices from the commercial world would almost certainly be beneficial.

Drawing on the experience gained from Bishop Birch's diocesan committees and their groundbreaking work, I pointed out that it was time for boards, associations, bodies, interest groups, businesses, individuals, families and communities to come together in a concentrated, co-ordinated and focused effort to drive Kilkenny forward.

> In my capacity as Mayor I can only help this process along, vocalize public opinion and provide a forum for debate. I will say what I feel has to be said and do anything necessary to promote the interests of Kilkenny. The formation of these action groups is one small step in that direction. I am launching into the arena people who are neither politicians or officials. By and large, they are business people, creative people, risk takers and decision makers. They have advanced themselves and are now willing to use their experience and give some of their time to Kilkenny in the best traditions of public service.

The Industry Action Group was established to consult with interested parties and outline the broad objectives for an industrial policy for Kilkenny City and county and had among its members Fergus Cronin, Joe Riordan, Kyron Crotty, Fintan Murphy, Brian Kiely and Gerry McGovern. The Film and Associated Industries Action Group investigated the feasibility of marketing and developing Kilkenny as a location for films, list the possible spin-off industries and research funding frameworks. Its members included Mike Kelly and Kevin Hughes of Young Irish Filmmakers, Richard Cook of the Cat Laughs Comedy Festival and Jon Hegarty. The Millennium Action Group was to propose ideas and co-ordinate the 2000 Millennium celebrations in the city and county with the support and involvement of villages and towns. It was to suggest methods of promoting Kilkenny abroad in conjunction with Bord Fáilte as the place to celebrate the event. That committee involved Eamon Langton, Carmel Costello, Zach Fahey, Richard Cook, Michael Lanigan and Dr Tony Joyce.

We also established working groups to lobby for a university in Kilkenny and one to guide Kilkenny's entry to the Telecom Éireann Information Age Town competition in which Kilkenny came a close second to Ennis. The work on the information age town project led directly to the establishment of the Maltings Enterprise Centre, which now houses the Chamber of Commerce and the studios of Cartoon Saloon, the animation company that was nominated for an Oscar for *The Secret of Kells*. The committees crystallised a sense of self-confidence and gave a shape and a face to what was happening in the community. Most importantly, they provided people with an opportunity to make a contribution.

I have no doubt that Paddy Donnelly was monitoring all of this work closely and recognised the difference in the way things were being done and how meetings were being conducted in a businesslike and inclusive fashion. He was certainly very accommodating with the requests I made of him since it was the first time we had a secretary in the office, computers at the disposal of the Mayor and a full-time active office that the citizens of Kilkenny could access—and they did.

THE FATHER McGRATH CENTRE: A MODEL OF SOCIAL ENTREPRENEURSHIP

Another opportunity to demonstrate the boundless potential of local communities helping themselves is the case of the Father McGrath Centre, which I had the privilege of opening with Prionsias De Rossa, who was Minister for Social Welfare at the time. It began as a building that had fallen into a bad state of disrepair to the point that the Corporation had taken a decision to demolish it. Meanwhile a young man called Stephen Murphy had returned from his travels to his homeplace in the Butts Green area of Kilkenny, long known as a proud but disadvantaged community. Steve and others appealed to the Corporation to allow a group of them to take over the building for use as a community centre and initially their request was rejected. However, after much persuasion by Steve and his colleagues, supported by me and others, the argument was won with the officials in City Hall and the Father McGrath Centre was born.

It no doubt had its roots in the earlier initiatives of Bishop Birch, Sister Stanislaus and others as was recognised when she was invited to open the Newpark Close facility. It was modelled on the Father McGrath Centre, which now stands as one of the finest examples of what is referred to as social entrepreneurship. There is a one-to-one homework club that helps keep children in education and gives them support and confidence in their abilities. There is a community centre that acts as a hub for the area and reaches out into the county too. It has become a blueprint for community-based initiatives, which has been recognised by FÁS, the Department of Education, colleges, schools and individuals throughout the voluntary and community sector. FÁS obviously learned nothing about how to build with little. This strengthened my belief that bureaucratic initiatives are largely a waste of money and dustbins of bad ideas. It is certainly the greatest example of community in action I have seen anywhere.

It proves the point that if you empower people and give them an idea that improves their lives and those of the broader community, they will rise to challenges and deliver results. For every €1 invested by the Government, there is a substantial multiplier effect on the local economy and more broadly in society. It also challenges us in politics and the public service to consider that, if we took the same approach to our work in local authorities and Government departments, so that people could see the range of possibilities, we could release that great latent energy to our great mutual benefit.

The new politics that we need in this country is about emulating the successes of the likes of the Father McGrath Centre by empowering people and communities at a national level as well as a local level. It is about making the Dáil and Seanad relevant and connected to the communities they represent. If we can achieve that, it will force a great degree of self-regulation among politicians. The closer they are to their constituents, the more accountable to them they are and the more transparent their work must be.

My own approach to public life, which developed through my years on Kilkenny Corporation and as a Mayor, encouraged me to go beyond the boundaries of narrow party politics. I think people in Kilkenny viewed me as one of their own regardless of their party allegiance and I was able to turn to them for guidance, support, opinions and assistance at election time. Despite some characterisations in the media, I am not an anti-establishment figure but I do have a mind of my own and a strong desire to promote changes that affect people's lives in a positive way. In the simplest terms that consists mainly of spending taxpayers' money efficiently and responsibly and giving value for money in the services we provide.

A MAYOR ABROAD

In November 1996, I invited the mayors of every local authority in the country to come to Kilkenny for a National Conference of Mayors with the aim of reviewing the economic situation at national and local level. A pretty bold statement, it was the first ever formal meeting of all the mayors of Ireland and there were a few raised eyebrows among the officials when it was initially proposed. However, as was almost always the case, once they saw the scope and vision of what could be achieved they rowed in behind the event to make it a huge success. We held the sessions in Butler House, the beautiful dower house of Kilkenny Castle, which is run by Kilkenny Civic Trust, another leading example of collaborative community and local government effort. We were heartened when every single Mayor who was invited turned up in full regalia to attend the conference, make their contribution and enjoy the occasion and the city.

Concluding my opening speech, I said:

> The people who elected us and the members of our Corporations, require that we be much more than figure heads. They want us to give leadership, overcome problems and find solutions. They are increasingly irritated by red tape and their representatives' inability to overcome it. In fact, if local government is to be credible and effective, officials and elected representatives will have to work in co-operation to create administrations that are efficient, transparent, professional and decisive.

In my view, politicians need to take risks and should be counter-balanced by officials, who are naturally cautious. This tension creates the essential dynamic in good local government or in any type of governance. Calculated risks must be taken, old orders need to be overturned when they have outlived their usefulness and creative co-operation must be allowed between the elected representatives of the people and the public servants who deliver to them. Unfortunately, newer public servants, perhaps because of rule changes, are risk-averse and will often seek to form committees when proposals are put forward rather than take crucial decisions.

I firmly believe that mayors should be empowered by legislation. All of them want to lead and come into office with a strong desire to make a contribution and a difference, in a way competing with the height of the bar set by previous mayors. They should be given the secretarial services and backup they need, because people do respond and much can be achieved at relatively little cost.

|THE THIRD MAN: ELECTED

MOMENTUM

By the autumn of 1996, it was apparent that my work as Mayor was meeting with a great deal of approval in the city and county, and appeared to be contributing to a positive atmosphere in the political life of Kilkenny. I began to believe I could run for the Dáil in 1997 with a real chance of success. The *Kilkenny People* and Radio Kilkenny had responded positively to my fresh and dynamic approach to the mayoralty and it was clear that the committees I had established were working well. I was getting good press and a positive public reaction. I was also enjoying every minute of it. I was a full-time Mayor getting things done and the results fuelled my desire to take my ideas onto the national stage. I began to make preparations for a Dáil election.

My family's history in Dáil elections had not been a happy one, but I was much more of a party organisation man than Mick. Although I am not a blind follower of anything, or anybody, I had served my time in the Fianna Fáil organisation and much of what the party stood for then was what I believed in. That, however, did not mean I would be nominated. It was certain that I would have to be added to the ticket by headquarters, who would consider me a 'sweeper' in the city for the two seats they expected to fall to the sitting TDs, Liam Aylward and M.J. Nolan.

That is what had happened to my father when he stood in 1961 after he had been added to the ticket by Sean Lemass. Jack Lynch added me to the ticket for local elections in 1979 and Haughey added me in 1985. I was selected by convention for the 1982 general election. In a rural constituency with dynastic families in control, Darwin rules: you get eaten or you get lucky. I fully understood why Liam Aylward and M.J. Nolan didn't want me on the ticket. I was a threat because of the success of my term as Mayor, which their well-tuned and efficient antennae had picked up. They would fight hard with the organisation to keep me out.

Liam Aylward dominated Fianna Fáil politics in Kilkenny and, having worked for him in elections, I knew why. His father Bob, a major figure in politics and the GAA, had unsuccessfully stood in three general elections before entering the Seanad in 1973. Liam worked long and hard across the county and built a powerful organisation to get elected in 1977 and in successive elections. He was elected as a Member of the European Parliament in 2004 and stood down from the Dáil in 2007, when his brother Bobby took the seat. Senator Michael Lanigan supported the Aylwards in Kilkenny, which was fair enough—he and Liam had been friends for a long time. That meant my base was weakened, which might be offset by the fact that the city traditionally votes for city candidates.

M.J. Nolan, again the son of a former TD, had County Carlow to himself, although I had my own ideas about that, but he was more vulnerable than Liam Aylward. He wouldn't welcome an add-on with a reasonably high profile. In short: my candidacy was about as welcome as a Blueshirt at a cumman meeting.

I would have to convince headquarters, fight the Aylward machine, upset M.J. Nolan, play a blinder and perform a miracle if I was to run and win. My late mother, God bless her, began doing laps on her rosary beads.

Then an omen of good fortune appeared at the kitchen window one morning when my father and I were discussing battle plans. It wasn't recognised immediately, because it came in the form of a political rival within Fianna Fáil whose relationship with our family was captured by my father's immediate reaction:

'What does that bollocks want?' The 'bollocks' in question was Pat Millea, a farmer from Tullaroan who had played the role of the third man in the elections of 1987 and 1989, performing very well on both occasions. He had beaten me in the 1985 County Council elections, when we exchanged hard words about the canvass.

His appearance at the window was mystifying, although neither my father nor I let that show, my father adopting the mien of a cat watching the behaviour of a troublesome Jack Russell as Millea entered the room. He was a county councillor and he had done his best to get to the Dáil, but he had reached the point at which he realised that was now over. That did not mean, however, that he had lost his competitive streak, his instinct for politics or his desire to break the Aylward hegemony and do his best for Fianna Fáil. Pat was and is a good party man. He had seen the profile I had achieved, done the numbers and decided he was going to be a kingmaker. He told me he would support me and offered me his hand. Mick remained fully convinced that the Jack Russell's only purpose was to fill the house with political fleas. I didn't agree with him.

Pat Millea was a poker player, had an astute political mind and a big support base in north Kilkenny. Furthermore, it took a strong man to do what he had just done. I shook the hand that more than any other got me elected and so began a friendship that I enjoy and value to this day.

SELECTION
Pat Millea's proposal was a novel one: he would get all the prospective candidates for the third place on the ticket for the next general election into a room and discuss and debate until there was only one left standing. He wanted to create an irresistible consensus among the contenders and have a challenger for third place, which he believed would be me. John Coonan, Kevin Fennelly, Evelyn White, Jimmy Brett, myself and Pat Millea met and debated. The exercise was also a good one in that it helped

bury some old gripes and differences—being politicians we kept a few in case we needed them in the future. The last person standing was me.

The Fianna Fáil selection convention was chaired by Michael Smith TD, who spoke emphatically at the outset of the meeting that the business of the day was to select candidates with the full intention of winning three seats for Fianna Fáil in Carlow-Kilkenny at the general election. There was great cheering and shouting at that suggestion and people were on their feet. Smith followed this up by saying that the purpose of the convention was to select just two candidates, at which point a delegate from Carlow stood up and said to him: 'Typical Fianna Fáil—we'll win three seats but we'll only select two candidates—by Jaysus, you're some mathematician.' General uproar ensued, but only two candidates, Aylward and Nolan, were selected.

The refusal to select a third candidate at the convention was largely driven by those who didn't want an addition to the ticket, namely Liam Aylward and M.J. Nolan. They wanted a weak sweeper rather than a strong performer and to ensure that only they as outgoing TDs were selected, giving them the opportunity to take their argument for a weak sweeper to Dublin. This they did, but I took my counter-argument that we could elect three TDs. Fortunately, Bertie Ahern and the party strategists shared my view.

Fianna Fáil was in Opposition at a difficult time for the Government and opinion polls indicated that we stood to pick up seats across the board. I was identified as having a strong base within the city and, as a result of the mayoralty, a wider profile in the constituency. Against that, there would have been major objections from some in the party hierarchy, urged by the Aylwards in particular. Nevertheless, Bertie Ahern had a singular focus and goal: Government.

At a meeting of the National Executive Bertie Ahern announced that the two outgoing Carlow-Kilkenny TDs would be selected for the general election and that John McGuinness would also be added to the ticket. 'Are we all agreed?' asked Bertie. The Executive did agree. I had the nomination to stand for election.

CAMPAIGN

My campaign began in January 1997 outside the Avalon Hotel in Castlecomer in north Kilkenny. Standing in the snow with Castlecomer party stalwart James Dormer, I was doing a live interview with Sue Nunn for Radio Kilkenny by mobile phone. 'And where are you this morning, Mr Mayor?' asked Sue. 'Well,' I said, 'I've started my campaign.' 'But it's snowing,' she said. 'That's right,' I said. 'I'm out here in 'Comer.' 'And you're going to canvas?' she asked. 'Yeah, I am—a good start is half the work.'

At that point I began to really believe that I might have a chance of being elected to the Dáil. The impact of the mayoralty had spread outside the city into north Kilkenny and, because I now had the support of Pat Millea, who was a powerful political force in the area, my possibilities were enhanced. I'd sensed the mood for change in the people, which was reflected in the theme of the campaign: 'Time for Action, Time for Change'. That change was about more than just changing the Government. At local level, there was a degree of complacency that assumed Liam Aylward, whose supporters canvassed everywhere during the campaign, would maximise his vote and be returned comfortably with Carlow TD M.J. Nolan.

A change in the approach to national politics by politicians in the constituency was also much needed and desired by the public. It was clear that we needed to emphasise to Fianna Fáil supporters that splitting or managing the vote would enable another TD to be elected. One of the critical tools in the election campaign was the posters that we produced urging people to vote strategically. This encouraged people to engage with the voting process.

The principle of asking supporters to vote strategically assumes that the candidates will divide the territory of the constituency equally and fairly between them, but these agreements are almost always more honoured in their breach than their observance. As well as being driven by a love of democracy and a desire to represent people in one's national Parliament in pursuit of the common good, it will come as no shock to readers to hear that politicians are also driven by ego! This means that not only are they content to be elected, they must be elected on ever greater numbers of first preferences. In multi-member constituencies, sitting TDs will jealously guard their support base and constantly seek to expand it, even at the expense of colleagues from the same party: Darwin in action.

We were making a big effort to upset this status quo. Family, including my father and mother, relations and friends and many canvassers were out in force. Pat Millea and Pat Fitzpatrick were covering a huge amount of ground and I was visiting more doors than the post office. I was getting considerable media coverage because of the nature of the campaign I was running. The work I had done as Mayor was paying dividends. I was working night and day in an attempt to knock at every house in the constituency and Pat Millea was working his heart out in north Kilkenny on my behalf.

Out in Tullaroan, Millea was never off the phone, either calling supporters or beating me up. 'Where are you now?' was the familiar question, followed by: 'You're not doing enough—you missed six houses there.' He was like the drummer on a Roman trireme and the beat was quickening all the time.

Finally, in the last days of the campaign, to the fury of my running mates, we put up our special posters, which said boldly: 'We can win three seats. Vote Strategically. Vote McGuinness No. 1 in North Kilkenny'. We signed it with the Fianna Fáil logo. There was murder, particularly from the Aylward camp, which had always won a big vote in north Kilkenny. The loss of some first preference votes as a result of people voting 'strategically' because of our suggestion was not appreciated, but that would not stop Liam from topping the poll. In the meantime, we kept going and going.

ELECTED

Horseracing is a great community occasion. There is something for everyone: runners and riders have to be considered, form has to be discussed, teeth sucked, views taken and bets placed. Finally, there is the excitement of the race and the joy and sorrow of the result. It's rather like the day of a count, in fact.

I do not know of what happiness-hoover thought up the idea of electronic voting. Most likely, it was an official who didn't like the messiness and humanity of the count, or the fact that for a few days in the country, politics comes really close to the people. Maybe they thought it would be that object of desire lusted after by some politicians and officials: a legacy.

It was a legacy all right—a legacy of incompetence and huge expense, created by bureaucrats far removed from reality and the people who were not stopped by their Minister. I cannot believe that any politician would want to kill the count. I certainly don't.

My day of the long count started on the morning of Saturday, 7 June 1997, when my family and supporters gathered in St Canice's Hall. As always, there was an expectant tension and electricity about the place as the other candidates arrived. There were soothsayers and tallymen everywhere and nobody really believed that I could make it. Too big a jump was needed and the early advice from the tellers as the count began bore this out.

But then it began to emerge that veteran Labour TD Seamus Pattison had polled very badly in the city and M.J. Nolan was also struggling. Liam Aylward, of course, was already out of sight. The tellers balanced this by saying that, as sitting TDs, Pattison and Nolan would do better in the county and I would be pipped at the post in the final shakedown. Nails were being hard bitten by my supporters and my mother's beads were steaming. On it went: box by box.

In the middle of the hubbub of speculation, calculation and wishful thinking, Dick Dowling, a former Fine Gael TD, called me to one side and said: 'Young man, you'll be elected today.' I asked him why he believed that. 'In every polling station out in the county, even in my neck of the woods, you're picking up ten, twelve and twenty votes. Your name is appearing in second, third and fourth preferences right around the county. Any man that can do that,' he said, 'is on the way to election.'

The first count elected both Liam Aylward and Fine Gael's Phil Hogan, their having reached the quota, and revealed that I had polled 5,990 first preferences, 400 ahead of Seamus Pattison and 15 more than my party colleague M.J. Nolan. It was critical that I stay ahead, at each stage, because you never know when a batch of transfers might just go wrong and put you on the losing side so it was a nerve-racking wait. As the count continued, we all edged closer to the winning post. Eventually, after the seventh count, it was all down to the transfers of Mary White of the Green Party, who had been eliminated. I edged in front and, after the eighth count, along with John Browne of Fine Gael and Seamus Pattison, I was declared elected, just ahead of M.J. Nolan who lost his seat.

After over 100 years of trying, a McGuinness had become a TD.

This had not been expected and a great cheer went up from my supporters. I was a bit stunned myself. I had been elected despite history and the Aylward machine and it was a moment to savour. There were many tears, my father was delighted and my mother took to saying thanksgiving rosaries.

I couldn't squeeze through the crowd so I vaulted the table to take the microphone. I gave Jack and Mick their dues and reflected on the foundations built up by Jim Gibbons and Senator Mick Lanigan that had led to a Fianna Fáil candidate from Kilkenny City taking a seat for the first time ever.

Reflecting on my election in 1997, it is clear that Pat Millea's support for me was a huge factor, but there was also the response of the people to what was a new approach to politics. I had told them that I would do my best and that I was asking them to vote for me because of my passion and ability rather than promises. They understood that and I continue to honour their trust.

The people had spoken, happily through the ballot box instead of the machine. I was on my way to the Dáil and I was looking forward to the challenges it would bring.

ENTERING THE DÁIL

As I came through the gates of Leinster House on the first day of the Dáil in June 1997, I did think for a moment of Jack and Mick, both of whom had tried and failed, but maybe it is our genes that make us eternal, so there was a little of them coming in with me. I hoped not too much! I could see how they might spoil my enjoyment.

The challenge did not daunt me. I had already been in politics for nearly 20 years by that stage and I knew the ropes. Furthermore, because of my membership of Fianna Fáil, I already knew many of the politicians in Leinster House with whom I would be working. All of that would count. I had no illusions about the political system or how difficult it would be to make a mark. I wasn't entering a monastery. I was entering an ego reactor.

As a member of the local authorities, I had dealt with civil servants at city and county level as well as at planning authorities, health boards, Government departments and the multiplicity of boards and quangos that administer the country. As a member of the Fianna Fáil National Executive, I had learned the internal workings of a political party and, as a businessman, I had very specific ideas on good management, governance and value for money, which I was determined to deliver to the people I represented.

George Lee did not know the ropes and, because of that, made his abrupt exit from the Dáil in February of this year having served just over six months as a TD for Dublin South. In an ego reactor only the experienced and hardened egos reach critical mass. George was an economics editor and a national broadcaster but he wasn't an experienced politician. From the Press Gallery in the Dáil, politics looks easy—the set pieces during the Order of

Business, the Second Stage speeches and the amendments to legislation on Committee Stage. But what happens in the Dáil chamber is not really politics. It is the result of politics.

Real politics happens in the hallways and offices, at meetings and functions around Leinster House and in one's own constituency. It's about quiet words in the ear, a meeting with a Minister, it's about deal making, back-scratching, the ebb and flow of allegiances and promises made and sometimes broken. What we see in the Dáil is essentially like a professional wrestling match. The moves have all been worked out in advance and name calling and chest beating are obligatory.

The parliamentary party meetings of the various parties are where policy and positions are discussed and debated. The parliamentary party meetings of the Government party is of course the most important of these because that is where TDs debate with ministers and argue over issues that may well become law. The public generally does not realise the importance of these meetings, which are held behind closed doors. In the past few years particularly, the Fianna Fáil parliamentary party meetings have been tense affairs with TDs frequently at odds with their ministers over legislation. These private discussions are a mine of information for journalists but, with so many whisperers, it is often very difficult for them to get the true story. Like many TDs, I frequently read articles, based on reliable sources, which are so wide of the mark, you'd wonder whether the whisperers were there at all.

It is actually quite difficult for an ambitious politician, which most TDs are, with a desire to make a difference to come into the Dáil as a member of the Government party and discover that a click of the Taoiseach's fingers is the difference between the great opportunity of a ministry and life as a vote on the back benches. It is, of course, also difficult for the Taoiseach. I believe his task would be made easier if political imperatives took second place to the needs of the country when appointing ministers, and committees were beefed up to give backbenchers more scope and power and important work to deal with.

All that and more was in front of me in June 1997 and I was excited about it, eager to begin work and make my mark. There were great expectations in Carlow-Kilkenny and I had every intention of keeping the only promise I did make: I will do my best. I went through the gates knowing that I had the experience, ability and energy to deliver that come what may.

Much of the first few weeks was given over to familiarising myself with the procedures, settling into my office in the Dáil and extending my office in Kilkenny to meet the demands of the constituency. An efficient, trustworthy secretary is the cornerstone of a good constituency office. I was lucky at an early stage to find Ann Bergin, who has remained with me and has proved a loyal and hardworking colleague, without whose help I simply could not get through the day, even though she fights with me from time to time. I was ably helped in turn by her assistants, Catherine, Anita and Lorraine.

In the early days, I was extremely grateful to have the help of my constituency colleague from Kilkenny City, the veteran Labour TD and later Ceann Comhairle, Seamus Pattison. He was generous with his time and shared with me his enormous knowledge and experience of the place. Outside the cut and thrust of the day job, or maybe because of it, politicians across party lines tend to get on well together. Seamus was a city man and he helped a fellow city man. Roots count. And so do second and third preference votes!

The late Séamus Brennan and I had worked together 20 years earlier in Mount Street headquarters on the 1977 election campaign. He was Government chief whip and we got on well together. He was also a great help. I respected the way he went about his business, confident enough to accommodate political differences but firm and fair when he put his foot down.

I was fortunate as a newly elected TD to be appointed to three interesting Oireachtas committees and to see how they work as part of the parliamentary system. From 1997, I was a member of the committees on European Affairs; Enterprise and Small Business; and Justice, Equality, Defence and Women's Rights. From a parliamentary point of view, I cut my teeth on these committees. Perhaps of most significance to me was my involvement in the Abbeylara investigation into the fatal shooting of John Carthy by the Gardaí. The committee ran into the sand as the limits of the system were challenged in the Supreme Court, which ruled that Oireachtas members had no role in making adverse findings about individuals. It is a ruling that has hamstrung the committee system since and one that must be addressed if we are to get the full potential value from our committees.

While working on the Enterprise and Small Business Committee, I was involved in the investigation into the insurance industry, led by Senator Donie Cassidy, which had been identified as overcharging Irish consumers and businesses to an outrageous extent, increasing vastly the cost of doing business here. As a result of the investigations, we were able to make recommendations that have helped to progressively reduce the cost of insurance in Ireland over the past 15 years.

Having been in politics for so long, it was not that difficult to fit into the pattern at Leinster House once I fully understood the procedures. It was an exciting place to be at an interesting and exciting time in our economic development. But, as we all know now, excitement has a price.

Chapter 6 ~

A PUBLIC SERVICE

CLIENTS AND CLINICS

The late great leader of the Labour Party, Frank Cluskey, once remarked that when TDs see constituents in their regular clinics, they encounter three types of people: one-third who'll ask you to do something impossible, another third who'll ask you to do something illegal and another third who are just lonely.

In recent years something of a consensus has emerged among political commentators about the clientilist system of Irish politics. They believe politicians who are elected to the national Parliament spend a large part of their time tending to the needs of their constituents. The consensus suggests, among other things, that this system is somehow unique to Ireland and that it is of itself a bad thing. There is an assumption that in Ireland TDs who are elected to Dáil Éireann should spend much more of their time working on legislation and making speeches in the Chamber on the burning issues of the day rather than engaging with citizens and helping them solve their problems. The argument also suggests that the serious concerns of people are somehow unworthy of the attention of a national politician and that this work should be done by councillors as members of local authorities.

It goes against the grain to suggest this but, to my mind, this argument has a number of serious flaws. First is the assumption that TDs have a significant role to play in legislation and the daily affairs of the House, which demands their undivided attention. The reality is that backbench TDs, unless they are members of the select committees, have almost no role in legislation, nor is it necessarily desirable that more than 100 of them should. Most TDs, on the Government side at least, understand in time that the best way for them to influence legislation is through raising a debate within the parliamentary party and seeking accommodation with the relevant ministers.

Second, there is an assumption that the problems and crises presented to TDs at their clinics by constituents can and should be dealt with by local councillors or the relevant Government agencies. Again, this is flawed for two reasons: the power and authority of councillors has been so diminished by the Local Government Act 2001 and the County Managers Act that they are no longer significantly involved and, most importantly, the problems that arise are more likely than not caused by the inflexibility or incompetence of those very Government agencies. Government in Ireland has recently become centralised to such an extent that it has vastly increased the distance between politicians, the citizens they serve and the officials who rule. This is not a good thing.

We have to remember that the 'clients' in the clientilist system are citizens like you and me. They are voters and taxpayers and the State, through its arms of Parliament, Government and local administration, is obliged to deliver to them the public services for which they pay in a fair, cost-efficient and competent manner. For the most part, the problems that are brought to me by my constituents arise because the State and its agencies are failing to serve the citizen. The system is failing the people who pay for it and it is the much-maligned clientilist system that has to pick up the pieces. If our public services operated as they should in a modern, citizen-focused, flexible and businesslike fashion, there would be little need for these clinics and TDs could spend much more of their time on the affairs of State.

The other important point to make is that it is these very clinics and the general interaction with the people they represent that keep politicians grounded and in touch with what is happening in the community and more broadly in the country. This is a vital connection and one that ensures that the real problems and needs of citizens are addressed by law-makers and administrators. The ending of the dual mandate, which forced TDs and senators to surrender their local council seats, together with the increased powers given to the bureaucracy by the Local Government Act, has eviscerated the traditional power and authority of local councillors and tipped the balance away from the public representative in favour of the bureaucrats.

I am not persuaded that a national Parliament of 166 thoughtful but disconnected legislators poring over the fine detail of the Industrial and Provident Societies and Friendly Societies (Miscellaneous Provisions) Bill is really what people want or need. That said, I would welcome reform of the Dáil and Seanad that placed a much greater duty on public representatives in the oversight of public bodies and Government decisions. What we do need is an administration that is fit for purpose and embodies the true letter and spirit of the term 'public service'.

Since TDs and senators ceased to be members of local authorities, the conduit that provided analysis, experience and an understanding of legislation has been removed. Councillors are now informed by the City or County Manager and the officials who are firmly in charge. They control the message and the information to the local representatives so that they are effectively sidelined into voting for the County Manager's orders or not. And bureaucracy marches on while democracy is ground down.

Every day I see people who are in desperate need of advice and guidance. Something has gone wrong and they come to me as a last resort. These people are being failed by our system. That is all the more obvious when it transpires that all it takes is a phone call or a letter from me to solve the problem. The reality is that the issues raised by constituents are brought up because of a failure of the system of government, either at local, agency, departmental or central government level to respond adequately to the needs of citizens.

People can no longer communicate with Government because it has become too big for them and too remote. For instance, a large number of the people who come to me are from marginalised, low-income households, non-nationals and Travellers trying to be housed by the local authority. They are given a 21-page application form to fill out and they are bewildered by the entire process. They are encouraged to complete applications online, yet many, such as the elderly, do not have basic computer skills or access to the internet. The system, we are told, is being optimised for the information age but it is skewed to the benefit of the public servants rather than the citizens.

When I'm dealing with a particular case with a constituent, I work with them to explain the situation and encourage them to understand the issues and take action themselves. In many cases, I will help draft a letter of appeal or complaint in the person's own name and introduce it with a letter from me. This is informed out of respect for the people involved. It is a core principle of mine to help people help themselves rather than assist in perpetuating a nanny state and a culture of dependency.

That dependency is frightening. There are swathes of families now who have never worked and their children surely will not work. I have watched these families start their descent from hard-working, honest grandparents to grandchildren and great-grandchildren who now know more about the social welfare system than I do. They now believe they have a right to expect the State to give them houses and support without any understanding of where the money comes from. This is the consequence of handing out money to people without thought or care as to how we might ensure that they get an education that, at least, teaches them how to stand on their own feet.

Reductions in benefits, like the Jobseeker's Allowance, are going to cause trouble, particularly now that there is no work. Having paid enormous sums out to create dependency, we will now have to pay even more to break it and develop a model that brings abandoned generations of lower- and low-income families into what we must make a more caring society.

The network of citizens advice bureaux around the country do valuable work in assisting people but they are limited in the scope of the advice they can offer. Politicians have a deep understanding of the systems, personal relationships with officials and the insight to interpret rules and regulations for people who are having problems. We can also take the initiative and take up particular cases in a proactive way when it is obvious that a person is being mistreated by an arm of the State. This is what I regard as real, representative democracy, which binds politicians to the people they represent and seeks to hold accountable the public servants who are ultimately employed by the taxpayers.

THE PUBLIC SERVICE

The public service in Ireland is made up of civil servants who work in the departments of Government and public administration through the various arms of the State at national and local level as well as direct employees of the State, such as members of the Garda Síochána, teachers, nurses, doctors, prison officers and so on. The system we have is largely based on the British model we inherited on Independence and the original staffing model was based on encouraging well-educated people to help organise the administration of the new State against a background of economic crisis and general chaos. Recruits were encouraged to join the service as patriots for the common good of the country and because the pay was relatively poor, extra incentives were added to the package. Civil servants were offered security of tenure in their position and pensions that were intended to supplement the modest wages they earned.

In the intervening decades, those elements, which began as simple and effective tools to recruit the best people to serve the State, became institutionalised and formalised assumptions about the general pay and conditions of civil servants, jealously defended by the public service unions. The problem is that the modest pay that required the perks grew exponentially as the State developed and the Civil Service expanded. In more recent years, the benchmarking process increased public sector salaries by significantly more than in the private sector. The theory was that these pay rises would be met by radical reform of procedures and processes within the Civil Service. This did not happen.

According to recent Central Statistics Office (cso) figures, average earnings in the public sector as a percentage of those in the private sector have grown from 113 per cent in 2000 to around 122 per cent in 2010. In their June 2010 report, Davy stockbrokers found that average earnings in the public sector were more than €43,000 a year, compared with a figure of €33,500 in the private sector. The cso also tells us that average weekly wage rates for the Civil Service almost doubled between 2000 and 2008, from €573.57 to €916.08. Despite the tough pay cuts and pension levies, the gap between public and private sector pay has been widening rather than narrowing.

That said, there are many people in the public service who earn relatively modest wages and salaries and the average is clearly skewed by the huge numbers at middle management grades. Between 2000 and 2008, the actual number of people working in the public service grew by a staggering 15.5 per cent.

These pay figures may also be distorted by some of the excessive salaries and bonuses at the top level. Heading the list is Padraig McManus, the ceo of the esb, who, while hiking prices to domestic customers and struggling businesses, is paid €420,993 a year as well as other perks, bringing his total package to around €750,000—almost twice the salary of the President of the United States! That comparison is often carried too far, but in this case I will let it stand.

He is joined by other high-rollers on the State payroll, such as former CEO of the HSE, Professor Brendan Drumm, who got a total package worth €600,000, including a bonus that, in the face of growing public disquiet about the state of the health services, he donated to charity. The CEO of the Dublin Airport Authority, Declan Collier, despite plummeting passenger numbers, enjoys a salary and benefits worth €638,000 a year; and another CEO of a State-owned utility, John Mullins of Bord Gáis, is paid €259,000. It must also be particularly galling for lower-paid public servants to hear that none of these CEOs were subjected to the pensions levy that was applied to them.

These salaries are exorbitant by international standards for public sector roles and are not justified in the kind of economic crisis we are now experiencing, particularly when many of the people who command these sums run organisations that have been slow to reform and are not giving the taxpayer value for money. The reforms and improvements in the delivery of public services that had been promised in the various reviews as a quid pro quo for benchmarking have failed to materialise. In that context, I very much welcome Brian Lenihan's decision in August 2010 to order a review of the salaries of semi-State CEOs and to appeal to them to take a voluntary pay cut in the interests of the country and to show solidarity with others.

In his Government-commissioned report on Public Numbers and Expenditure, the economist Colm McCarthy identified savings of €5.3 billion to the Exchequer, including the cutting of 17,300 staff working in the public service. While this seems like a huge number of people to take out of the system, mainly through voluntary redundancy and non-replacement, it has to be considered that some 15,000 extra public servants were employed in just the three years to March 2008.

According to the OECD's *Towards an Integrated Public Service* report in June 2008, the Irish public service:

...is a reflection of national political and administrative cultures, and of past economic and social priorities. It is clear from studying the Irish system...that there are difficulties involved in leading system-level change, and in pursuing system-wide coherence. If it is to maximise the public service's contribution to achieving these societal objectives and to meeting citizens' expectations, then it needs to think increasingly about the Public Service as an integrated 'system'. In doing so, it will have to amend or revise existing account-ability structures and ways of working, to allow for integrated system-wide action where this is required.

The OECD report is dense and heavy on jargon and is loathe to be explicitly critical but its recommendations for reform are clear and if one reads between the lines the current system is not working at all as it should. It calls for improved governance and performance dialogue, including the sharing of information and the increased use of external expertise; and networked approaches to working in the areas of agility, informality and openness. It recommends moving towards a performance focus by intro-ducing more measures of outcomes; and prioritising spending within budget frameworks, taking a strategic, long-term approach to budgeting. It says the public service should use e-government to deliver integrated and citizen-focused services, the full potential of which is not being realised because of the use of fragmented ICT systems.

The report found that there is an urgent need for the increased use of open recruitment to the public service in order to rapidly acquire the necessary skills and competencies that cannot be easily located or grown in the short term among the existing cohort of generalist public servants. Despite the obvious need for professional expertise in the public sector—particularly during a time of crisis—between 2005 and 2009, the Top Level Appointments Committee, which deals with recruitment to secretary general, deputy secretary and assistant secretary grades, held 82 competitions for positions involving 300 candidates and appointed just one single person from outside the public service. In answer to a parliamentary question tabled by Richard Bruton of Fine Gael, the Minister for Finance confirmed that in 2007 there were 106 applications from outside of the public service for top Civil Service posts; there were 150 in 2008. In 2009, the number of such applications fell to 33. People obviously got the message that no outsiders need apply.

The OECD report recommends that 'the development on a phased basis of a single, integrated public service leadership cadre, through the creation of a senior public service with a membership drawn from elements of the broader public service, would allow Ireland to strengthen a system-wide perspective at leadership level and to reinforce core values through the public service'. This is simply common sense that just requires the joined-up thinking between departments that has been a feature of corporate and business environments for decades.

The report also says that strong leadership at political and administrative levels must move from the traditional position of control to one that emphasises vision, support and direction. And it points to the need for increased flexibility and mobility for workers. Evaluation of performance and targets it also underlines as being particularly weak in Ireland.

Most importantly, it states that the success of reform of the public service depends on changing behaviour, which is dependent on rethinking how the public service operates and putting the conditions in place to change behaviours. This, to me, is the key point. The public service is a system and it is a culture. My criticisms of the failings of the Civil Service and public service are of that system and that culture and not of the individuals involved.

THE DEPARTMENT OF FINANCE

In a series of articles for the *Irish Times* in April 2010, eminent management consultant Dr Eddie Molloy was fiercely critical of the Civil Service and the Department of Finance in particular. He pointed to a document on the Department of Finance's own website: the Annual Outputs Statement for 2009, which he described as 'a comprehensive, succinct list of everything that has catastrophically gone wrong'.

The document sets out the Department's 'central role in the economic and financial management of the State and the overall management and development of the public sector' and boasts about the Department's outputs under the headings of five high-level goals. According to the Department's own evaluation of itself, it delivered on every item—economic growth, sustainable employment levels, competitiveness, value for money from public expenditure, supply of credit to business and personal customers and 'an efficient and high performing public service and improved levels of service to the public'. I think most of us would beg to differ on the Department's self-assessment in more than one category.

The Department of Finance is particularly important to examine because it is ultimately responsible for the staffing of the public service. And despite its glowing end of term report for 2009, as Eddie Molloy points out, the Department has in this role:

> ...provided 'best advice' that has delivered bloated public service staffing, unsustainable pay and pensions, massive upward grade drift, system-wide rigidities, abuse of flexitime, high rates of absenteeism, and weak management. To this we may add the degradation of the capacity of the public service through decentralisation, which against all reason it is still pushing through; utter failure to deliver on the long-promised reform of the public service; a set of guidelines which provided cover for the scandalous exit package for Rody Molloy; and

most recently, the ill-advised reversal of pay cuts for assistant secretary grades.

A damning indictment indeed.

The Department of Finance has also been accused, correctly in my view, of failing to recruit and retain the best external experts in economics, auditing, accounting and cost-control not just in Merrion Street but across the public service as a whole. This has led over the years to waste, cost-overruns and outright incompetence in the delivery of public services and capital expenditure. The use of external consultants has also exposed the taxpayer to potential conflicts of interest and excessive fees. Instances of these abuses of taxpayers' money are revealed in the annual reports of the Comptroller and Auditor General and further elaborated on in the Public Accounts Committee to which I will return in Chapter 8.

The practices that have been allowed to obtain in the public sector—in Government departments, semi-State bodies and various quangos—would not be tolerated for an instant in the real world of business and must make our system of public administration a source of ridicule in corporate boardrooms around the world. Worse than the ridicule, however, is the deep concern that one must assume that potential investors looking at the waste of public money endemic in the system will wonder what we would do with their money if we care so little about ours.

The self-assessment of the Department of Finance is worthy of satire but the effects of its failures on society are no laughing matter. The continuing practice of one insider replacing another in the succession to the top positions in the Department—as happened when Kevin Cardiff replaced David Doyle as secretary general in 2010—ensures that the culture of the place sustains itself, closes itself off from criticism and creates its own echo chamber in which real change is fiercely resisted. Indeed, it was commented on by a former official that an economics degree was actually a barrier to promotion within Finance. Eddie Molloy again puts it well when he describes the problem as similar to that which is convulsing the Catholic Church.

> The problem is deep and goes right to the top. The high priesthood of the Civil Service has its own moral code and an even greater facility than any bishop for using mental reservations to obscure the truth. They are all intelligent and decent people, but they are trapped in a disastrously dysfunctional bubble, blind to their own shortcomings and failures.

Of course, all of this is compounded by the fact that senior civil servants are practically unsackable, a condition that is intended to protect them from political interference but also means that they are unaccountable for their decisions and actions to the public they serve. When they come before Oireachtas committees such as the Public Accounts Committee, these officials are prevented by the Ministers and Secretaries Act from making any comment on policy or on advice given to ministers. They are also given anonymity in reports that are critical of decisions and actions of their departments.

With the introduction of the Freedom of Information Act as an attempt at some degree of transparency, some civil servants took to writing the phrase 'not a document' on certain pages so that they could not be officially requested. This fundamental lack of accountability and transparency in how our system of governance operates must be changed if we are to develop as a twenty-first century society and economy. It is patently obvious that self-regulation does not work in any sphere of modern life and there is no reason to believe that the public service is different, despite the use of the meaningless PMDS (Performance Management and Development System) process that was offered as a quid pro quo for the excessive benchmarking pay awards of the past 10 years.

The announcement last summer by the Minister for Finance of

an independent review of the Department of Finance to cover the systems, structures and processes used by the Department in its role advising the Minister and Government was a welcome one. However, its scope is not nearly wide enough. The review must also be extended to all functions of the Department, including its role in the recruitment of personnel and the management of the wider public service. Other similar reviews should also be carried out on all departments of Government, beginning with the most crucial economic department, Enterprise, Trade and Innovation.

VITAL REFORM

It is not enough that we hand money over and hope that enough gets to the public. As politicians, it is our responsibility to ensure that it is distributed efficiently and cost-effectively. It is also our responsibility to ensure that both politicians and the public get service and respect. But the machinery we are using is obsolete, slow and tired. The public and many civil servants are calling for a modern, efficient system that gives satisfaction and a sense of achievement to those who operate it and a speedy, friendly service to those who use it.

We badly need a Minister for Public Sector Reform with a seat at the Cabinet table and a remit to work across all departments with all the stakeholders to bring about the cultural and institutional transformation that has long been promised but not delivered. The public service unions, particularly those that represent the top echelons of the service, need to examine their role in a new economic environment. The hangover from the social partnership house party has to be dealt with aggressively but constructively. And now is the time to do it.

An infusion of fresh blood is needed to begin to change the embedded culture. We need to provide much better quality and specific training for civil servants—training that is important and central to their work and that reflects best international practice in the private as well as the public arena. We need strong

independent leaders who are prepared to work with Government to refocus and energise the public service, not just for the good of the country but for the morale and fulfilment of civil servants themselves. This reform agenda needs to be seen as a positive approach to improve the working environment of the officials who work there rather than an attack on them.

A change of culture could become an engine of economic expansion and an international model of best practice. We need to release the potential of people to perform at a high level. Our system of government depends on a tension existing between the political and bureaucratic arms of the State. The former deals in the short term and can be impetuous; the latter has long-term goals and can be too cautious. At best, the tensions should act as a brake on one and an accelerator on the other. I believe that tension has not existed for some time. The arms are acting independently of one another and politicians and the country are the losers.

Government itself says: 'In the Irish system of public administration, government departments are, and should be, the primary locus of public policy formulation, evaluation and analysis. Policy evaluation and advisory functions should not, as a general rule, be carried on by external state-funded agencies.' This is hard to square with the continuing existence of an estimated 800 quangos, and with the many consultancies in the public sector.

It is essential that we restore the tension between bureaucrats and politicians. An arrangement whereby they get on with their job and we get on with ours is not good enough. In the end we are in charge and we are responsible. We have allowed too much power to slip away from us as representatives of the people. The pendulum has swung too far and it's time we restored the balance.

Chapter 7 ∽

BEYOND ACCOUNTABILITY

*I cannot accept your covenant that we are to judge
Pope and King unlike any other man. If there is any
presumption, it is the other way, against the holders of
power, increasing as power increases...power tends to
corrupt and absolute power corrupts absolutely.*

LORD ACTON

Over the course of my 30 years in politics, I have
encountered almost every aspect and level of the public
and Civil Service, from local authorities, through State
agencies to Government departments, from the point of view of a
public representative advocating on behalf of citizens. To follow
on from my comments about clientilism in Chapter 2, I must
reiterate that I would not have to engage in this work if the system
worked properly. Therefore, in my view, it is the dysfunctional
and unresponsive system of public administration that is the root
of the problem and should be the focus of reform. I want to
outline some of these particular cases, which are notable by the
extraordinary efforts made by certain officials in moving
mountains not to help solve problems but to protect themselves,
their Department or organisation and perpetuate the system that
caused the problem in the first place. They are also important
because they underline a growing trend towards a place where the
public and Civil Service is beyond accountability.

The Office of the Ombudsman in Ireland was first established
in 1984 with Michael Mills in the first role. The purpose of the

office is to investigate the administrative actions of Government departments, the Health Service Executive (HSE), local authorities and An Post. By the end of 2008 approximately 72,000 valid complaints had been handled by the office and it deals with up to 10,000 queries from the public every year. In her 2010 report, the current Ombudsman, Emily O'Reilly, accused the HSE of being riddled with secrecy and acting at times in its own self-interest and she said that her office had considerable difficulty accessing records held by the HSE.

The Ombudsman received 2,873 complaints in 2010, the highest recorded in over 10 years, more than 25 per cent of which related to the HSE and its services. During one investigation she described her office as having been led on an 'Alice in Wonderland trip' around the legal system as the HSE tried to prevent a report being published. She said:

I think there is a huge issue around the excessive secrecy and legalism of the HSE and it strikes me that it is a cultural thing within the HSE, and it is redolent of a body that looks not to the public interest, which is the only reason it's there, and seeks at times to protect its own interests and that's very wrong.

'It's as if the HSE lives in a parallel universe,' she added, pointing out that others, including the Minister for Children and the Government, had not been able to secure information from the HSE recently in relation to child deaths in care. 'So there is something rotten within that system,' she said. Of the other complaints to the Ombudsman last year, 41 per cent were about the Civil Service and Government departments and some 30 per cent about local authorities.

A SICKNESS IN THE SYSTEM

The HSE was established by the 2004 Health Act, and came into operation on 1 January 2005, replacing the 10 regional health boards, the Eastern Regional Health Authority and various other bodies that delivered health services in the State. The health boards themselves had been established under the 1970 Health Act, which radically reconstituted healthcare provision in Ireland from a largely private and voluntary system, principally run by the Catholic Church, to one that operated at a regional level, under the aegis of the Minister for the Environment and Local Government and overseen by boards that comprised a chief executive, local politicians, other elected representatives from medical practitioners and pharmacists, and public servants.

The health board system was often accused by critics of being subject to political interference, whereby decisions that should be made on operational or medical grounds were overridden by decisions made on grounds of political expediency under pressure from the politicians on the boards. That said, the local boards did provide genuine oversight and accountability at local level, where problems could be identified locally and solved locally.

However, the health boards had too many members, a top-heavy management structure and totally inefficient overlaps and duplications in terms of their administration structures. When the principle of the HSE was first proposed I was very supportive of it, because it was intended to rationalise the system to deliver a more efficient and cost-effective health service. I looked forward to a streamlined service that would maximise resources at the front line of healthcare delivery and eliminate the layers of middle management that had grown unchecked over time.

Unfortunately, however, the promise of the HSE has not been realised because the existing layers of bureaucracy were actually retained and added to, rather than stripped out and reconfigured. The political will required to take on the vested interests of the medical profession, the unions and others was sorely absent. Indeed, the massive centralisation of the health services by the HSE has created a monster that has perpetuated many of the bureaucratic ills of the old boards and has removed a direct democratic link between people in the community and those services so they have no influence and no comeback when things go wrong, as they often do. One need only read the cases outlined by the Ombudsman's report to assess the lack of accountability and transparency at the heart of the system.

Another stated goal of the abolition of the health board system in favour of a centralised HSE was the reduction of costs and the application of efficiencies in the system, an ambition that frequently finds its way into official presentations, which more often than not becomes an expensive own goal. However, the budget has now ballooned to a staggering €16 billion, up 400 per cent since 1997, and yet Ireland's health service is still ranked 24th out of 33 European countries in terms of value for money, according to the Euro Health Consumer Index (EHCI).

Colm McCarthy's report on public service numbers, commissioned by the Government, recommended cutting 6,000 jobs from the health service in order to save €1 billion, but this has been rejected by management and unions. In its attempts to centralise and streamline the delivery of health services, the Department of Health has instead added another layer of wasteful bureaucracy with less and less accountability and transparency to the public.

That layer of bureaucracy is a growing annoyance to frontline workers in all areas of the public service, who can see for themselves the problems and expense it is causing. For instance, nurses could run hospitals better than those who now give them instructions and would be paid for it if the bureaucrats were not in place. 'Bring back Matron' should be their cry. Yet unions cynically use frontline public service workers, like nurses, when they protest about change. But I believe the day is coming when frontline public services workers will refuse to allow themselves to be used to cover waste and overstaffing at middle management levels, which actually endangers their jobs and prospects.

And still serious systematic problems come to our attention through the media on a weekly basis. The health services are naturally a focus for public concern because of their ability to generate emotion in dissatisfied users of the service. This often results in big and truthful headlines directed against the Government, because it is 'responsible'. In so far as the Government has overall responsibility, that is true, but as with so many State organisations now, it is powerless to bring about the rapid and wide-ranging changes needed. For a plethora of reasons, one of them being 'beyond political influence', the tail now wags the dog. And it is a very big tail. I have attempted to pull it on a number of occasions, with varying degrees of success. It needs to be docked. But that is illegal nowadays and its trade union protectors have an aversion to blood-letting, which sooner or later they will have to get over.

Mary Harney is doing her best in difficult circumstances. She is a Minister for whom I have considerable respect. She has an intimate knowledge of her brief and has chosen to work in a Department that most politicians would run a mile from—Brian Cowen called it Angola. But her hands are tied. If you can't move the unions you can't change the Department. Mary Harney does not get enough credit for the changes she has initiated, despite this handicap. My experiences are tiny beside hers but may serve to highlight the mindset that she faces every day.

SOUTH EASTERN HEALTH BOARD

In mid-2001, I was approached by a son whose elderly and terminally ill father could not get a bed anywhere to afford him some comfort and dignity at the end of his life. This case again raised an issue on which I had been campaigning for many years, namely the lack of adequate or appropriate care for elderly people in Kilkenny.

I wrote to John Cooney, the then CEO of the South Eastern Health Board, seeking a meeting to discuss the provision of long-stay places for the elderly in the region. You might expect that as a local Dáil Deputy, I would receive a phone call to set up a date and time for such a meeting. You would be wrong. Instead, by return correspondence, John Cooney enquired by way of a multiple-choice question which model of care I proposed or had in mind. I responded with another request to meet face to face to talk through the options informally and confidentially and was again parried with a request for confidential details of the family concerned. I was unable to persuade him to meet me.

Subsequently, at the July 2001 meeting of the South Eastern Health Board, Mr Cooney raised on the agenda the issue of 'The Board's relationship with TDS'. He said that my request for a meeting with him had been 'concurrent with a story run in the *Kilkenny People*' and that he had received correspondence from me that he said: 'seems to suggest a role by him in relation to Health Board policy and the discharge of my role as Chief Executive Officer'. He said that those two matters were 'reserved functions of the Board' and that he did not wish '...to create confusion by giving the Deputy the appearance of any such function in the system which would appear to undermine the board's own position or draw the public's attention away from the board's central role'. He also claimed that I had 'recently sought an extremely high profile in relation to health issues in Kilkenny' and that he did not wish 'to be drawn into an increasingly political environment as the general election approaches'.

This is just a standard version of the 'electioneering defence' that is regularly used by State officials. In this case, like many others, it was entirely untrue. I had been interested and active in health board matters even before I became a TD.

Cooney's proposal, which was accepted unanimously by a compliant board, a number of whose members were local politicians, was that he decline my request for a meeting: 'a request no other Deputy has made to me. I am also aware of the need to treat all deputies equally. I will, of course, accord the normal working courtesies for Dáil deputies to Deputy McGuinness in relation to representations he may make on behalf of citizens.' In his subsequent letter to me, the CEO stated that it was his 'policy to brief Dáil Deputies collectively from time to time'. At that point, four years after being first elected to Leinster House, I had not received a single invitation to such a meeting. So much for policy.

The condescending message I was being given was that I had no role as a public representative holding to account public servants providing taxpayer-funded services and that when I attempted to address complaints about the services brought to me by those same taxpayers I was merely electioneering. To me this was and is totally unacceptable in a democratic society and an insult to the democratic process itself. It was variously claimed that I had invented the case to seek publicity, that I had no role in representing the community, that there was little wrong with the services provided and that everything was fine—carry on as normal.

Two full-time public relations specialists were employed by the health board and they seemed to spend a great deal of their time handling complaints about services, denying anything was wrong and defending a dysfunctional system. They busied themselves undermining my position and defending the health board, leaving me wondering how the health board could afford, and why it needed, two expensive professionals at a time when patients were being treated in corridors.

All of this culminated in a letter from the chairman of the South Eastern Health Board—and Fine Gael Mayor of Waterford—Hilary Quinlan, accusing me of 'reprehensible and unacceptable conduct' by making 'an unwarranted intrusion into the affairs of the board in relation to which you have neither mandate nor competence'. He said that the board had asked him to convey to me 'our desire that you should cease your attacks on the board and its officials and instead attend to your role as a TD in a manner which is not injurious to the board and its interests'. In other words, as a public representative I should only represent the public as long as it did not upset the delicate sensibilities of public servants in the health service. Needless to say, this was not going to be how I went about my job. And it shouldn't have been the way Hilary went about his job either.

This episode is indicative of what happens when one takes on a deeply ingrained and embedded system that has lost sight of its purpose. The people who work within the system are not bad people, but they have become victims of a sort of Stockholm syndrome in which they are hostages to and defend to the last a greater power upon which they depend. Any criticism, even if it is demonstrably justified, is treated as an attack on the hive instinct of the organisation and it reacts like the proverbial hornets' nest. In trying to carry out my duties in representing the public interest, I became the enemy.

Public representatives are accused of electioneering, bullying or acting outside their authority when they attempt merely to ask questions of public servants about the services they provide. Instead, we should be treated as potential partners in the community, who can provide client feedback on services, communicate procedure and policy to the public and act as good agents in the delivery of services to the citizens. Also, of course, on the boards, politicians should remember their role is to stand outside the prevailing culture and make sure it is responsive to the needs of the public.

DÚCHAS

In 1996, Dúchas was formed by the Heritage Act as an executive agency of the Department of Arts, Sport and Tourism to take the functions of national monuments and historic properties and the management of national parks and wildlife from the Office of Public Works (OPW). It was subsequently abolished in 2003, but not before it had engaged in some of the worst instances of wasted money, inefficiency and lack of transparency that I have experienced in my time in politics.

I was once told by a man experienced in company takeovers that one of the problems he always encountered in the course of that work was 'sacred mysteries'. He said there were always individuals or a group within the acquired company telling you that you can't really understand what they are doing and the company will fall apart if they are not allowed to continue, their way. Investigating this claim almost always resulted in the discovery that 'sacred' was there to deter and obstruct close inspection and the 'mystery' was how they had got away with wasting so much for so long.

The State apparatus is full of sacred mysteries and guardians, now still only being gently probed by Dáil committees finding their feet and gaining confidence, but Dúchas was in a class all of its own, because in dealing with ancient buildings and artefacts it not only had sacred mysteries but a secret language: mullions, guarderobe chutes, crenellations, portcullis, dollied, quoin and batter have the ability to quickly dampen the enthusiasm of a half-hearted interrogator.

Actually, Dúchas was in the building and artefacts repair and conservation business. Its work can be easily understood, even if the cost of it usually beggars belief. For instance, there is little or no difference between pointing a modern wall and pointing a Norman wall with generally a four and a half to one ratio of sand to lime—the things politicians learn—but 'Norman' tends to divert your attention while substantially increasing the price. A good mason should do around 12 m of pointing a day.

I did these calculations for the work done externally on Reginald's Tower in Waterford and began to wonder if they had also re-pointed St Peter's in Rome. Dúchas received good press, because of its trophy buildings like Kilkenny Castle, Reginald's Tower and the Rock of Cashel. It was an esoteric branch of the State tree that looked good but had never been shaken. In fact, as I was to discover, it was poorly managed, enormously self-satisfied and completely unused to any form of critical attention. But I did not know this when I started.

It began with Kells Priory, the largest medieval monastic settlement in Europe, which is situated on the banks of the King's River beside Kells village in County Kilkenny. The Kells community, under the leadership of an exceptional man, the late John Sheridan, had decided to use and celebrate the Priory by putting on a sculpture exhibition, which developed over the years into one of the major attractions of Kilkenny Arts Week, with up to 5,000 people attending. I became involved in negotiating with Dúchas, in whose care the Priory was, to help get this off the ground. Little work had been done on the Priory for a long time except for the erection of scaffolding, which by then had been there for so long that it could itself have been listed. I began to push Dúchas to take some action about the site, because Kells had given me an idea.

Kilkenny is a Norman city and county. There is a great number of Norman castles, keeps and buildings in various states of repair throughout the county, as well as notable pre-Norman relics. They deserve saving for their own sake, as part of our heritage, but sensitively used they could also be a working asset—a concept I don't believe Dúchas ever contemplated.

Throughout the world, there are families bearing Norman names and carrying the genes of those extraordinary adventurers. Some of them, like the Butlers, who visit Kilkenny as a group once every few years, have formed associations. I believed if proper professional marketing work was done on my idea, Kilkenny could be on to a winner.

The county could market itself as Ireland's Norman centre by creating a Norman trail between the buildings in the county, opening a Norman museum and, finally, a Norman study centre, which would not just bring long-stay tourists but students and scholars to Kilkenny. I wanted this to be a serious, grand enterprise and not a tourist trap. It was and still is a good idea that I regularly encourage politicians and officials in Kilkenny to act on. In fact, I wrote to Diageo asking the company to consider providing a site on the grounds of Smithwick's brewery to house the museum and study centre.

To investigate the possibilities, I asked my brother Declan, a stonemason and district foreman with Dúchas, responsible then for the care of its monuments in the south-east, to take me around sites in Kilkenny. The buildings, ruins generally, were powerful, beautiful and crumbling away into the ground. I still have the photographs and the barrage of parliamentary questions I raised in the Dáil about them are still on the record, as are the obfuscating, dissembling replies that Dúchas provided to me as a member of the Dáil.

I had a good idea and I wasn't going to let it go easily, but it was becoming more than that and I was getting angry with Dúchas. When the State is wasteful on a project it isn't just a matter of loss of money it is the loss of opportunity to spend that money on something else: more beds in hospitals, better social housing, better care for the elderly, more schools and better care for—and therefore, more useful—national monuments.

Dúchas didn't really see that—few State organisations do— and they didn't really want the public or politicians taking an interest in their secret society, or the way it was spending money. And the press wasn't interested—after all, politicians and promoters of clientilism and headline grabbing are much easier targets than State organisations. Only today is it beginning to become apparent that the press was chasing mice around the elephant in the room. The reporters I approached at that time were standing on the edge of a story that just grew and grew over the years.

I decided to become a busy mouse. I began to use an auditing approach to Dúchas: sample, discover errors, omissions and evasion, and expand the audit. I began checking what they were telling me and it was often wrong or inaccurate. I was told, for instance, when I asked about doubtful management control and accounting practices, that the internal auditing department had

Mick McGuinness congratulates Jack Magennis on being made Freeman of Kilkenny City, 1950.

From left: Town Clerk Peter Farrelly, Sean Lemass, Eamon de Valera, the Papal Nuncio Dr Alibrandi and Mick McGuinness.

1976: Fianna Fáil celebrating 50 years, with *second row*: Mick McGuinness (*extreme left*) and Tom Nolan (*fourth from right*); *front row*: Jim Gibbons (*extreme left*), Charlie Haughey (*third from left*), John McGuinness (*centre*) and Brian Lenihan Sr (*third from right*). (*Tom Brett*)

1979: Father and son make history: John and Mick McGuinness. (*Tom Brett*)

From left: John McGuinness, Paddy Carpenter and Jim Gibbons, 1982. (*Tom Brett*)

Mayor Kyron Crotty presents Mick with the Freedom of the City of Kilkenny, 22 September 1995. (*Tom Brett*)

Outgoing Mayor Kyron Crotty presenting the chain of office to John McGuinness in 1996. (*Tom Brett*)

St John's Cumann meeting, 1997: Nancy and May Murphy. (*Tom Brett*)

Enjoying victory in 2002.

A break from the campaign: (*from left*) Bertie Ahern, John McGuinness and Pat Millea. (*Tom Brett*)

From left:
Brian Cowen,
Mayor
Tommy
Delaney
and John
McGuinness.
(*Tom Brett*)

City Hall, home
of Kilkenny
Corporation,
now known as
Kilkenny
Borough Council.
(*Courtesy of
Kilkenny Borough
Council*)

investigated and found nothing wrong. Wow, that was that, then. Well, no. I was learning.

I asked about the qualifications of the people in the internal auditing section and discovered that there was no one with professional qualifications in an organisation spending huge amounts of public money, which rather took the gloss off 'Internal Auditing'.

Lack of fully qualified professionals is seriously damaging both the efficiency and reputation of our public service. These important positions are being filled by people moving up the promotional ladder. Often they are moved from positions that bear no relationship to the one they are about to fill, being moved from, say, auditing, to human resources—disciplines that require entirely different skills and personalities—because it is their turn to be promoted. God knows how many square pegs are now in round holes because of this union-supported system, which does neither the individual nor public service any good.

At this point I must say that trade unions supported all of this and must take substantial blame for the way the many good people in the public service, their members, were led down a blind alley, encouraged and seduced into abandoning common sense, their higher personal needs and their individuality for the false promise—the deadly promise—of security. The result in terms of morale, satisfaction, individual growth and vibrancy in our public services generally is a disaster amounting to human rights abuse.

My brother had laughed when I told him about my ideas for Kilkenny, telling me that Dúchas was a law unto itself and I wouldn't get anywhere. But he loved his buildings, and he began to help me, which didn't do him any good in the long run.

In the examples given below it should be borne in mind that while I was dealing with Kilkenny and the south-east generally on one level, my mind, as in auditing, was considering the bigger national picture and the cost. My examples are just that, taken from files, all of which I don't have time, space or energy to cover, but there are a lot of them and, elsewhere, almost certainly a lot more that I don't know about.

I discovered that there was a state-of-the-art computerised stone-cutting machine in the Dúchas yard in Kilkenny, which had cost €76,000. It was being worked manually. No one had asked the manufacturer to train an operator!

I was very concerned about the tendering procedures and controls generally in the Kilkenny depot, since considerable sums of money were involved. I was provided with an internal auditing report at one stage, in an attempt to staunch my questions. It referred to the values of the impress system used in the office, as if it were the Holy Grail. Maybe it was. The system is about 500 years old and it is used to control petty cash—and confuse pesky politicians.

It got better. I remember a meeting with the secretary general of the Department—arranged no doubt to get me offside or off the case or both—at which he told me blandly that the Department did not have records going back five years of the cheques they had paid to a company about which I was concerned, nor did they have ledger cards. But then it is only public money, I thought. I told him not to worry, that the company itself was legally bound to keep records for seven years and would, on request, have no option but to provide copies of its ledger cards to such a major client. 'Ah, no,' he said regretfully, he couldn't do that either! He had as much interest in helping me or investigating what I was concerned about as Brian Cody has in losing All Irelands.

Of course, this may not have been the case. Perhaps, when I left the room, he leaped into action, but I doubt it. Despite the fact that I had told him that I didn't want a witch-hunt and would be happy once any weaknesses in the system were corrected, he had shown no willingness to engage with me. I was a politician and I think the general public service position is that the less we know about, the better.

I am sitting across from a senior representative of this State, who is telling me that the State cannot account, and I am thinking, this is the State that makes hardworking people in corner shops around the country keep detailed records, employ accountants and pay every cent of tax due. 'Do as I say not as I do' is an attitude that sooner or later causes a rebellion. I left empty-handed and light-headed, but full of concern about actually how much this Department was capable of wasting. Later I was given a public demonstration at my own front door: Lacken Weir.

RIVER NORE FLOOD RELIEF SCHEME
Following a series of devastating floods in Kilkenny City in the 1980s and 1990s, there were frequent public calls for a comprehensive flood relief scheme that would anticipate and mitigate against the potential effects of the 100-year flood. As with any Government-funded capital investment, competition was fierce and Clonmel in County Tipperary was vying with Kilkenny to secure funding for its flood relief scheme, which it was hoped would prevent the arguably far more severe flooding in that town. However, Kilkenny secured funding for its scheme.

The River Nore Flood Relief Scheme in Kilkenny was a considerable feat of engineering and a world beater in terms of cost control and overspend. Estimated at €9 million, it ended up costing you, dear citizens, €49 million, a price that included the cost of miscalculation, arrogance and incompetence at Lacken Weir, which is on a scenic stretch of the river beneath the walls of Kilkenny Castle, a short walk from my constituency office.

It had been warned that the construction work would create serious disruption to the city, but the benefits were many and members of Kilkenny Corporation voted in favour of the scheme. Early tests in heavy rains proved the scheme to be a great success in preventing the type of flooding that had been experienced in the city for hundreds of years but there were some problems.

The consequences of the river having been widened and

deepened below Lacken Weir had been overlooked. This increased the height of the weir above the now-reduced water levels, preventing fish passing. The fish pass installed by the OPW was too steep for the fish to swim up, resulting in hundreds, if not thousands, of breeding salmon throwing themselves against the weir in a desperate attempt to continue the run to their spawning grounds. Many died of exhaustion and I nearly joined them as I tried to persuade the OPW and the equally bureaucratic Fisheries Board, which itself deserves close scrutiny, to listen to the fishermen's representatives.

The weir had become national news with pictures of exhausted and dead salmon. No one wanted a picture of an exhausted TD. Refusing to listen to Alan O'Sullivan, the river specialist employed by the fishermen, who was recommending a rock ramp, the OPW messed around with the first pass and built another. They were determined that the State would not be proven wrong. Neither worked.

I sought the help of my friend and colleague, Noel O'Flynn TD, then chairman of the Joint Committee on Communications, the Marine and Natural Resources. He brought a delegation of the committee to Kilkenny, listened to the fishermen and called all parties before the committee and told Sean Benton, the chairman of the OPW, to work with O'Sullivan to remedy the problem and that if it didn't happen he would be called back to explain to the committee—political decision making at its best. A rock ramp was constructed under O'Sullivan's supervision and is still working perfectly and may be replicated elsewhere.

Someone had made a mess of the original construction, either through incompetence or carelessness, and was never penalised for it. The State paid much more for the weir than had been budgeted—money that could have been saved if officials had listened to O'Sullivan in the first place—and killed God knows how many breeding salmon in the process.

BULLYING

Meanwhile, Dúchas continued to impede, confound, deny and annoy me as I looked behind ancient walls and checked ever more ancient and unsteady financial practices and foundations. Later I was told confidentially by a senior employee that the organisation was getting desperate about my questions and beginning to fear that it would be the subject of an internal audit and that I was within an inch of uncovering significant weaknesses in their control systems. When the OPW came before the Public Accounts Committee it emerged that I was largely on the right track.

In a very familiar pattern, the officials responsible would not accept responsibility for the mistakes nor would they concede mistakes had been made until they were forced to do so—just as the National Roads Authority (NRA) would pursue a project without due regard for the concerns of the community and other stakeholders, make mistakes for which they did not own up and spend a fortune in taxpayers' money remedying their errors, all the while denying anything was wrong or that the system was anything but perfect.

But that did not stop the main door in Reginald's Tower in Waterford being closed for four months because of what Dúchas, in a reply to a parliamentary question, referred to as a 'rogue stone' (a stone they had not noticed), which had not been taken into account when drawings for a new door were being prepared. They didn't tell me that the principal reason was that it hadn't been noticed that the floor wasn't level, leaving a €2,000 door lying unused in the Kilkenny depot. The exterior pointing in the building had cost a small and, my investigations showed, unnecessary fortune. But as one door remained closed, a dump opened.

In June 2003, as a result of information I had received, Dúchas was caught dumping waste in a scenic fen under its protection in Killenaule, south Tipperary. The investigation that followed revealed that 4,000 tonnes of waste, which I believed contained asbestos, had been secretly dumped over four years. It was also revealed that 250,000 colour brochures had been dumped because they had been over ordered. An interesting question would have been by whom and from whom, but by then the questions were piling up.

The report on Killenaule was conducted internally, of course. Up to today, it remains a mystery who found the site, made an arrangement with the owner, ordered the lorries, paid for the work, recorded the transactions and authorised the operation. It was no surprise to me that it did not find anyone responsible for the illegality. Nobody—useful tools of justice, internal audit reports.

Funnily enough, though, within a year the man who blew the whistle wasn't working for Dúchas any more. Just went. Another mystery.

Do not misjudge or underestimate the diligence of the servants of the State, backed by your money when it has to deal with troublesome TDs and dissenting voices within its ranks. Dúchas was as fed up with me as I was with it. As I began receiving and using more and more information from my brother and, separately, from other Dúchas workers around the country, it started to get into gear. Nothing illegal like dumping, of course, nothing personal—just due process in the service of the State.

Bullying within closed reactionary cultures is a standard tool used to stifle dissent and individuality. I have had quite senior people in my clinics from the HSE and other State organisations suffering from its effects. It is difficult to come to grips with, because it begins with a gentle push on a lever, a nod or a blind eye from a superior, a quiet word or a nasty whisper and suddenly, out of nowhere, an individual's life is made miserable, that which he or she believed was benign and protecting becomes unstable, threatening and sometimes vicious. Union representatives, themselves a part of the collective, don't quite represent, which is shameful.

The individual is isolated, outside the herd and often has a mental breakdown. Usually all the person has done is resist bullying, question a practice or a superior, show a flash of individuality, or begin to believe that there is a better, less wasteful way of doing things. In short, he or she starts to think and begins questioning the operations of an organisation they may have worked for all their lives, which in itself is a traumatic event for the 'company' person. Finally and reluctantly, a case of bullying may be taken against the organisation. What happens then is interesting.

Sometimes a bullying claim is made against the person who made the first bullying claim. Nudges, winks and pushes become more serious. Statements are taken and an employment law assessor, appointed and paid for by the State—upon which his company usually depends for much of its work—starts an investigation. I am not saying that the assessor is anything other than objective, but the claimant, by this time, is unsure and wary of anyone employed by the State.

Very often the process overcomes an already stressed individual, rather like discovery does in legal cases. The case is then dropped and the person leaves, probably never to work again. Early retirement is another option or, for the very determined, continued employment within the organisation, which is generally guaranteed to ensure that you are never allowed to forget that you are not welcome.

In the course of preparing for this book, I spoke to a number of people I represented or advised in bullying cases over the years. They were happy to talk to me, but none wanted their names mentioned. Even those who had left State employment were so damaged by the experience that they remained fearful of the State's capacity to cause them trouble. Two cases are sufficient to demonstrate what I am talking about. One of them does not want his name revealed and the other one is my brother.

The first is a man who came to me because he was worried about waste, lax controls and management in an OPW depot. He was a decent, committed tradesman who could not tolerate what he was witnessing. He raised his concerns with management and, in a State reaction that I had become familiar with from other cases, he was stonewalled and quietly put on a watch list. Levers were gently pushed and his working life was turned into a nightmare.

As a result of coming to me, his complaints were investigated and some action was taken against others, but he was ostracised. Unable to sack him, because he had done nothing wrong, the State simply put him in an iron mask and, for eight years now, he has for one reason or another been denied the opportunity to have a normal working life, often being given demeaning or trivial tasks to do, while at the same time being subjected to official work reviews, which I believe are being used to create a file that will one day be used against him.

As a member of the Irish Parliament, I am ashamed of what my country is doing to this man's life. Also, I feel responsible because, confident of justice, I encouraged him to challenge, instead of telling him to keep his head down, probably because I had never seen any value in keeping your head down. I did so not fully understanding how brutal and reactionary the State can be and how it will callously, but legally, sacrifice the lives of people and deny them justice in the interests of control and example.

I met a number of senior civil servants in my efforts to get justice for this man, against whom, I emphasise, no accusation of wrongdoing has been made. They listened and left. They should be ashamed of themselves. They have nothing to be proud of about the way he and his family were and are being treated, using due process. Neither should anyone in a senior position who does not now take action to make sure he is given back his life.

My brother Declan does not mind his name being used and I do so only because I want to put a face on this abuse and drag it into the light. There are too many people in State employment living in fear and silence, because the cost to them of standing up is too great. But this is a cancer that not only affects their lives, but the lives of those who are pressed into enforcing it and those in control who turn a blind eye to it and, ultimately, the reputation of the State itself.

Declan loved the opw and the building he looked after as a master stonemason and district foreman. He had started with the opw as an apprentice stonemason and he believed absolutely in the organisation until he began to distrust the culture and question the practices. When we began visiting the sites, it was clear to me that Declan was unhappy and disenchanted with the way the organisation was doing its business. I was with him in that, having already experienced Dúchas's indifference. He provided me with information and pointed me in several right directions but it was, of course, obvious to the organisation that this was the case. Levers were lightly touched and we were away again.

Declan's area of responsibility was reduced from the whole south-east area to Kilkenny only and then, in a two-fingered gesture in my direction, renovations in Kells only. He was left waiting in Kells for a number of weeks before he was provided with the necessary huts and when they arrived, one of them had 'F--- you' painted on it. While he was there, his office was cleared out and the usually subtle techniques were applied to diminish his status in the eyes of his fellow workers. Ridiculous requests were made of him, which, as was intended, would be hard to believe if he repeated them.

This was an organisation to which Declan had given his life and he suffered greatly from its withdrawal from him. He had a breakdown and then lodged a bullying and harassment claim that was given the full nine yards by the Department, leaving no stone, rogue or otherwise, unturned: professionals were employed, statements taken, etc. etc. Declan, exhausted by the amount of concern being shown, couldn't take it and left the organisation. He had done no wrong.

Legislation giving protection to whistleblowers, particularly in State organisations, will not work. They will be got at in ways that are difficult to predict and impossible to prove. A whistleblower may complain once or twice about it to, incidentally, a State organisation, NERA (National Employment Rights Authority), but the cost in time and stress will get them in the end. Look at the man I have spoken about above. His work is being assessed, but it is impossible for him to fully explain how he is being prevented from discharging his duties properly. For instance, he is asked to write reports, but not given enough information or support. Pity about that, bit of a black mark there! He gets someone, like me, to represent him and we are told he is just making excuses! I believe the Ombudsman's office should supervise bullying cases involving the State, because no whistleblower will want to deal with any State organisation run by officials, like NERA. Within a month or two of a whistleblower's name becoming public knowledge, they will not want to touch the State.

As vice-chairman of the Public Accounts Committee under chairman Michael Noonan, I arranged to bring the OPW before us to deal with waste and mismanagement. There were some stormy meetings in which I expressed my concerns in a very direct manner. Michael Noonan decided to arrange a meeting between himself, myself and the chairman of the OPW, Sean Benton, in an attempt to resolve the differences, which was fair enough. Michael, wanting to get the meeting off to a reasonable start, said something like 'Sean, you're doing a great job but there are a few questions here and there, nothing more than you would expect with a big organisation.' His intention was to bring me onside. 'That's more or less it, John, isn't it?' said Noonan. 'Not really,' I said, 'it's not.'

I turned to the chairman and said: 'Sean, I have to tell you that I think your organisation is a poor manager of Government resources. The taxpayer would be angry with you if they knew exactly what was going on with their money.' I went through every individual case and told him that the next time the OPW came before the committee, he could expect an even more robust exchange of views. 'OK,' said a disappointed Michael, 'that's an end of this meeting.'

Síle de Valera, the Minister then responsible for Dúchas, and I had a terse correspondence regarding the organisation. She told me, more or less, that her Department was providing me with all the information I needed and she copied her letter to Bertie Ahern. In my reply, I fully outlined to her my concerns and pointed out that as the Taoiseach had an accountancy qualification it would be easy for him to understand what I was talking about.

In 2003, Dúchas as an agency was abolished and subsumed back into the OPW with elements of it transferred to other departments. I have no reason to believe that the waste and incompetence stopped and I'm pretty certain the bullying hasn't either. I have no intention of stopping because I believe the people of Ireland should know why €49 million was spent on a project costed at €9 million, without anyone really being held to account; why the State organisations can escape the same external auditing procedures that private companies have and why the State can use its power and public money to silence dissenting voices.

Those who might be inclined to believe or want to believe that the cases I know about belong simply to the tiny minority of cranks who work for large organisations are wrong. I am no fool. The many I try to help but do not name are the tip of the iceberg. There are a great many good people in the public service who suffer in silence or speak out in vain, their lives and individuality crushed by the State and the unwillingness of unions to disturb a comfortable arrangement for the sake of an individual or a group. If that is overstating the case a little, it is because of my anger that so little is being done to open the corridors of the public service to modern human resources thinking and workplace practices and the winds of change, excitement and challenge.

My scrutiny of Dúchas and the OPW lessened around 2004. There is only so far you can go—and the State knows this—

without public, political and press support. It is a pity, because closer inspection of this wayward child of the State might have revealed enough to encourage a closer look at some of its bolder siblings and relations, persuading politicians and the media to take a stand to stop unnecessary and sometimes scandalous takes from the public purse.

My experience with the Oireachtas Committee on Communications, the Marine and Natural Resources in the Lacken Weir case, however, gave some cause for hope for the future. The committees of TDs and senators of all parties can and could work very well and achieve real results for people if the respective chairs push out their parameters and, as Noel O'Flynn did, act like the national figures they are and flex their muscles on behalf of the citizens of the State, holding to account the departments and public bodies over which they have purview. This was in stark contrast to the Oireachtas Joint Committee on Transport, which refused my request to inquire into the Donal Norris case even though it could have done so if it wished. And had it done so, it could have saved this man and many others in Ireland a considerable amount of anxiety and pain and, at the same time perhaps, put manners on the people they were dealing with. That is what committees are there to do.

The sad reality is that, because of the behaviour of a number of venal politicians, public representatives are not trusted to have any influence over, for example, road-building or flood relief schemes or how local health services are delivered. This power should not be vested in unelected, unaccountable bodies, often with compliant boards that do not question. To me the direct connection between the work of the State and the people for whom the work is done is the essence of democracy. People need to have watchdogs that protect their interests. That is one of the reasons politicians are elected and if they fail in that duty they should not be re-elected.

PARLIAMENTARY QUESTIONS

Parliamentary questions (PQs) are one of the most important instruments in a TD's toolbox and they save a great deal of Dáil time. They allow us to submit in writing specific and detailed questions of a Minister or Minister of State relating to issues of concern under their responsibility. They are answered by officials in his or her Department and placed on the record of the Dáil. A question is normally answered within three days and 90 per cent relate to matters that are not contentious.

The difficulty starts with the other 10 per cent, which may be probing a Department on issues likely to cause embarrassment. The answers then generally become oblique, obfuscating, incomplete, defensive and sometimes misleading—the officials involved in drafting the replies being more interested in avoiding the questions than supplying the information requested.

I have raised this matter a number of times and recently, Emmet Stagg, a Labour Party TD, again brought it to the attention of the Dáil. Our point is: officials of the State are answering questions in a manner that subverts the democratic process and TDS should be given the facts no matter how embarrassing they are. It is also true, of course, that incomplete answers are themselves a measure of the State's regard for democracy. I believe the Ceann Comhairle's office should take a much stronger line with complaints from TDs about inadequate answers and lift the bar by referring the questions to the appropriate Dáil committees to pursue if necessary.

There is also the peculiar fact that ministers are told that it is not the done thing to ask PQs in the normal way. I don't know why this is but they are expected to write to the relevant Minister with their questions. Bizarrely, the reply can take more than two weeks!

Frustrated by this, I wrote to a number of ministers pointing out that ministers must surely be entitled to the same prompt response as TDs. I received exactly the same reply from each Department, so obviously the officials had talked to one another.

They were happy with a system where an acknowledgment is issued in three days and a comprehensive reply within 15 days!

Those targets are rarely met, so, with the same question, there is a lower standard for ministers than there is for TDs. I just don't understand why officials don't handle all the questions with the instruction that they refer trickier, if indeed they are, ministerial questions to their superiors.

This is just a tiny example of the widespread unwillingness to make any changes towards best practice and, because of this, as usual the arrangement has been sidestepped. Many ministers simply ask a party colleague who is a TD to ask the question on their behalf!

DONAL NORRIS

In the introduction to this book, I outlined the case of Donal Norris, which, more than any other, informed my views about the dysfunctional relationship that exists between the State and its citizens in modern Ireland.

The building of motorways and dual-carriageways in Ireland began when billions of euro in European Structural Funds were allocated to the purpose in the early 1990s. These funds were administered by the NRA, a semi-State body, which is beyond political influence, and spent by local authorities that were largely the same. The local authorities were responsible for planning, engineering and procurement and dealing with the many families affected by the road-building programme.

Land was compulsorily purchased at a standard rate per acre and, while there were objections, many families like the Norrises accepted that the roads were being built for the common good and accepted the process, requiring only fair and reasonable treatment and a modicum of sympathy and understanding of the frustration, inconvenience and change that they were having to deal with. They did not get it.

The Norrises were bullied, put through bureaucratic hoops and forced to the point of exhaustion to fight for their rights and common sense. They were not alone in their community and elsewhere in the country. Hundreds of people had the same experience.

Essentially, I think the huge sums of money and the grand scale of the road-building programme went to the heads of all the participants and mere mortals and their concerns were pushed to one side and ignored as the God of Projects became careless about where he was putting his feet, making the NRA and Council impossible to deal with.

For some time before he came to me, Donal and his local community had been talking to Kilkenny County Council about the Council's plans for the Piltown/Fiddown bypass, a 9.3 km stretch of roadway that was going to be built beside them in south County Kilkenny. They had a number of concerns.

The plans showed that the road would run within 35 yards of his house and would bisect his 50-acre farm and separate the community and there was a number of other farmers in the same position. Planning arguments revolved around 12 right-hand turns that did not have any ghost islands, access for cattle and machinery on divided land and, of course, the route the road was going to take through farms. A flyover that could have been put where it would connect most of the community was placed where it served only a few houses. Water from the road ran into fields and turned them into swamps. In addition, Norris and his community wanted acknowledgment and respect for the huge upheaval in their lives.

They got nowhere, their objections largely ignored by the Council engineers, officials and the NRA, which were funding the project. Essentially, I think the huge size of the road-building programme nationwide had numbed those responsible for it to the grief, anger and sadness being caused to those families unfortunate to be in its path.

Norris and his group decided to lobby local councillors, TDS and MEPs and their concerns were raised at meetings of Kilkenny

County Council and reported in the media, but politicians could get no response from the system and consultants. For Norris and his group of protesters, the situation worsened. The road was now designed to come within a few feet of the Norrises' house; access to Fiddown and Piltown became more dangerous because of the poor design of an underpass that was restricted to one car at a time, thereby preventing its use by the school bus, which now had to take a circuitous route. Better alternative proposals by the community were ignored.

Around the beginning of 2001, Donal Norris sought my help in the campaign against the design and for his rights as a landowner. His wife Patricia and his mother told him not to bother. They felt bullied and intimidated, had no faith in the system and were exhausted by the struggle. Donal decided to try one more time and he came to me. I looked at the plans, listened to him and was concerned and I called to his house a few days later to see for myself.

There are two elements to the story of Donal Norris and his community. First, their genuine concerns and good alternatives were never really considered during the planning process. Second, the compensation payments had to be expensively argued and they had great difficulty getting remedial work, like paths, underpasses, etc. completed. There was really no financial compensation for damage to the quality of their lives.

The community had lost confidence in the whole process even before the work had begun because of the arrogant position of the State. It is not unreasonable to expect in relation to these huge projects that the State puts appropriate people in place who specialise in anticipating and resolving conflicts of this nature and to deal with the pressure on people and communities who have no experience of officialdom. Neither engineers nor Council officials are psychologists. Norris and his community were concerned and distressed about what might happen to them and their families at every stage of the process. They were right, but it was not pleasant to watch.

The Norris family was certainly feeling the pressure. They were in despair and, together with the community, up against the power of a State, the goodwill of which they had taken for granted. They had been fighting the planning process for two or three years and were exhausted. The road had cut the farm into a 30-acre plot beside the house and another 20-acre plot on the other side of the road. They had lost 7 acres and the road was above the level of the house, 15 feet away, with only a fragile timber fence separating them from the noise and a possible runaway vehicle. Cups were rattling on the sideboard with the vibrations of the passing traffic as I sat in the kitchen.

The Norrises were not the only ones affected. John and Kitty Byrne had lost 7 acres of their 30-acre farm to the bypass and the farm itself was cut in half. They were contemplating giving up milking, because they were afraid to drive their cows across the road. A request for a small underpass had been refused. An official had helpfully suggested to them that as they were getting on, they should give up farming! The Byrnes hadn't just lost land. They had lost a whole way of life and they now regularly drive a much-reduced herd across a busy motorway to access the other half of their farm.

Another elderly couple had 12 acres taken out of a 52-acre farm that was their life's work. It just went on and on. And it was happening all over the country, but the Norris case forced all of this into the open much to the chagrin of the NRA, which wasn't good for Norris in the long run. The pressure and anger created by the insensitive way this matter was being handled by officials was palpable.

During 2001, I used every opportunity to raise this matter at local and national level: I contacted the NRA, raised it in the Dáil and at parliamentary party meetings. The media began to take an interest and headlines appeared: 'David Vs Goliath at Fiddown' (*Kilkenny People*, 18 May 2001), 'People Rising Up' (*Kilkenny People*, 15 June 2001).

I was concentrating on the County Council and in June to July 2001, as I became more aggressive, there was growing interest across the country, more cases were emerging and I demanded detailed reports on the various problems identified by the community.

In November 2001, safety audit reports raised a number of issues. Norris and I continued the pressure and in an interview on Radio Kilkenny, I attacked the indifference, the procedures and the loss of respect for the lives of the people. And I called the road an 'engineering fiasco'.

Within a few days, a solicitor's letter arrived at my constituency office from the engineers' union. It threatened to take legal action for libel and said they would withdraw co-operation from me. I wrote back to tell them that Larkin and Connolly would be revolving in their graves at the thought of a union preventing a representative of the people from speaking out on their behalf.

This retort may not have been sensible, even if it was understandable. A union or a professional body representing a member knows that the threat of legal action, which they have the funds to pay for, is likely to push a TD off the pitch, no matter how good his case, because he may not be willing to risk the costs involved.

A special local council meeting was held to deal with all the matters pertaining to the road. Nothing happened.

On 21 October 2001, the *Farmers' Journal* ran the headline: 'The Wall of Official Indifference', and in the article, Donal confessed that 'nothing can prepare you for the stress and torment you will go through'. The road officially opened in early 2002 with the *Farmers' Journal* carrying the headline: 'Road Fiasco: The Cows Can't Come Home!'

Waiting for a decision on an underpass to get to his fields, Norris had to walk with his cows along the new road and through the car underpass under threat that he would be fined €1,000 for each day he did that. Gardaí acted as stewards along the route and

I joined Donal and the local community as they walked with him in protest.

On one occasion he was contacted by an NRA official who told him he would get no compensation if he continued to protest, probably because it was causing them trouble elsewhere. Donal asked the official to repeat the threat as the local garda was listening. The official hung up. Later he called back to check if the garda had, in fact, been listening! Internal farm cow lanes were the issue. Four of his nearest neighbours got theirs but not Donal. The protest lasted six weeks.

He had been milking 40 cows, but was now down to 20 because he simply couldn't manage the farm, the family and the fight. I continued to pile on the pressure, attending public meetings highlighting his case and advising other farmers in the same situation to visit Norris and support him.

In May 2003, I wrote to the Minister for Transport expressing dissatisfaction that my letter of December 2002 remained unanswered. No reply. The system wanted another man in an iron mask and Norris, because he had highlighted the issue, was seen as someone who should be made to pay.

In the end, Donal got his underpass and some other issues were resolved at considerable cost. But, even today, some parcels of land have still not been transferred and his money is still lodged with his solicitor. He had to complete fencing himself recently, at a cost of €4,500, as the NRA did not do the job. There is still work to be done by the NRA, like the knocking of a building on his boundary and the removal of trees, one of which was blown down recently and damaged his house.

The right-hand turns on the roadway that the community had expressed doubts about did not work. A number of people were killed before ghost islands were installed. The road is still being redesigned and retrofitted with individual solutions, but many problems still exist. Ten years have gone by!

Donal Norris stood up to a State that didn't care and in which he and his community believed and it cost him. The bigger picture is that his standing up encouraged others throughout the country to do the same. But did it teach the State a lesson? I doubt it.

Chapter 8 ~

| PUBLIC ACCOUNTS

The Public Accounts Committee (PAC) is one of the Irish Parliament's most important bodies, charged with the oversight and monitoring of Government expenditure. It is a standing committee of the Oireachtas, with a membership comprised of TDs only, and enjoys greater powers than other committees. In particular, it can compel witnesses to attend and demand that documents be furnished to it. It meets every week and considers reports by the Comptroller and Auditor General (C&AG), who is the Irish State's chief auditor. He or she is responsible for reviewing the spending of taxpayers' money to establish if value for money has been achieved. The committee reviews the C&AG's reports and questions the relevant departments, with officials from the Department of Finance, the overseeing department, to establish that procedures are in place in order to apply transparency and accountability to that spending.

The process is intended to reveal fraud, corruption, incompetence and negligence by reviewing past performance. The hope, which I do not share, is that the prospect of being brought before the PAC to explain huge holes in budgets, missing money or incompetence should be a deterrent to any future behaviour that treats tax euros as mere numbers on a page. Officials should feel the breath of a forensic auditor down their neck and fear the glare of publicity as they deal with billions of euro of hard-earned tax revenue. Unfortunately, the reality is that while they might feel the breath of the watchdog, they know that it has only a limited time to bark and it doesn't really bite.

The PAC's powers are not sufficient to deal with the sort of incompetence and negligence that would have an employee, no matter how senior, of any commercial concern out on the street with his P45 in minutes. There are no real sanctions. Officials who have been incompetent seem to be able to continue their climb up the promotional ladder without difficulty and the PAC continues to deal with the sins of the past without having the power to deal with the emerging problems of the present.

THE DIRT INQUIRY

The PAC has in more recent years begun to build a higher profile as a comparatively dynamic arm of the Dáil. We regularly see headlines that scream about waste of taxpayers' money and incompetence. The enhanced position of that committee in Irish politics can probably be partly attributed to the DIRT inquiry in 1999, which, for the first time, was televised live. The inquiry concerned the widespread and systematic avoidance by banks and their customers of deposit interest retention tax from its introduction in 1986 to 1998.

Part of the DIRT legislation in 1986 was meant to encourage non-residents particularly, perhaps, of Irish origin, to use Irish banks for depositing money, the interest on which would be tax free in Ireland. It is a moot point whether the Revenue was encouraging tax avoidance in other countries. If it was, it had even greater success in encouraging it in Ireland as thousands of Irish residents, sometimes with the help of their banks, became ghost residents anywhere they could find a suitable address abroad.

The DIRT inquiry became a long-running saga on TG4, attracting large numbers of viewers as the committee questioned bank directors and officials about their part in the scandal. It emerged that some bank officials had assisted their customers in organising addresses abroad and indeed had participated themselves. The inquiry also revealed not just the loss of tax due on interest but the use of the accounts as a means of concealing sums liable to a variety of other taxes. In fact, it marked the end of the Revenue's relaxed view on tax collection and began an era where it developed a model that matched and sometimes surpassed international best practice.

The Revenue's response was one that demonstrated the contribution the public service can make when it gets into gear. I reflected, at that time, that if the public service applied the same diligence to spending money as the Revenue did in collecting it, the country would do very well. Unfortunately, the Revenue's example was not followed generally by its siblings in the State sector.

But the inquiry also brought a huge weakness into the light. The PAC could and did force retribution onto the banks and individuals but it has never really been able to do that in the other direction when the State and its senior representatives are incompetent, lack professionalism and allow waste. What is sauce for the private sector goose should be sauce for the public sector gander.

Driven primarily by its chairman, the late Jim Mitchell TD, and Pat Rabbitte, a sub-committee of the PAC was formed to conduct the inquiry. The hearings, which began on 31 August 1999 and continued through the month of September and into early October, examined the State and its agencies, the financial institutions, their external auditors and the industry representative bodies. Some 142 witnesses gave evidence over 26 days. The enhanced powers of the committee under new legislation, the examination of witnesses under oath, the live broadcasts and the rapid publication of the proceedings all represented important advances in parliamentary scrutiny and demonstrated to the public that their Parliament could hold those in the private sector and individual citizens to account.

A NEW POSITION

I had been an active member of the Committee on Enterprise and Small Business while the DIRT inquiry was underway and worked with members of the PAC on various issues. I had obviously made some impact in my work and had garnered a reputation for close scrutiny, plain speaking and generally being a thorn, because immediately after the general election of 2002, Bertie Ahern phoned to ask me to take the position of vice-chairman of the PAC. Given that the position of chairman is traditionally passed to the Opposition, for a Fianna Fáil Government backbencher this was a great honour and responsibility.

The five years I spent as vice-chairman of the PAC reinforced the views that I had long held about the poor state of governance in this country, how taxpayers' money was not being properly accounted for and how the system needs a radical overhaul. The work in which we were engaged involved the examination of the operation of Government departments and the management of Exchequer funds. At one meeting, I reflected that money for the State was collected by the hard-boiled and spent by the soft-centred, which did not go down well with officials. It was clear there were insufficient controls and systems for counting money in and out across every Department. Nor did many have the management expertise necessary to count everything. In my view, what gets counted gets done.

As someone with a background in business, it was actually shocking that we would meet every Thursday to examine the poor conduct of expenditure within a Government Department that simply would not be tolerated for a second in the private sector. In fact, it would generally have bankrupted the business engaged in it.

Best practice in good governance is not applied across most Government departments, but they are still there because there is no real measure of performance and no penalty. When private organisations or citizens are found to have failed to account for expenditure or do not control budgets, there is always a penalty: the Revenue Commissioners, shareholders, creditors, customers or regulatory authorities may pursue them. But in the public sector when things go badly wrong, nobody is penalised because usually nobody is found to be responsible.

As a backbencher, I had already encountered many cases like the ones I described earlier, which caused me concern about how money was being spent by central and local government. I had made assumptions from my experiences but once I began to read the regular reports of the C&AG, it became clear that, if anything, they were optimistic. Every week a different Department or agency would appear before the committee to explain away wasted money, cost-overruns and poor accounting.

On 21 November 2002, the PAC met for its first public meeting of the 29th Dáil. Fine Gael's John Perry had been elected chairman at a previous brief session and the first item on the agenda was the election of the vice-chairman. Fianna Fáil Deputy Seán Ardagh nominated me for the position and I was seconded by Sean Fleming and duly elected vice-chairman. The earnest work then began. That first meeting of the PAC dealt with the administration of bail by the Garda Síochána and the Court Service on foot of a report from the C&AG that showed that less than 10 per cent of €640,000 in forfeited bail money had been collected. A €500,000 shortfall!

We heard from officials from the Department of Justice, Equality and Law Reform, the Garda Síochána and the Courts Service and it appeared that a lack of co-ordination between the arms of the State and an underinvestment in IT systems were at the root of the problem, raising questions about the quality of its manual system. It was a relatively minor issue in the overall scheme of things, but it underlined a lack of 360-degree thinking in public administration, which was to arise time and time again. It also showed a lack of foresight in the drafting of the bail legislation—by officials in the Department of Justice—that would enable a more efficient and effective bail system that would be taken seriously by those to whom it applied.

A SHORTFALL OF €2.5 BILLION

My first substantial engagement on the PAC, however, came in January 2003 when we met to consider the C&AG's reports into the Department of Finance's accounts for 2000–2001. This in itself demonstrates one of the serious weaknesses of the PAC as an effective oversight and audit body for the public finances. It is limited to the discussion of reports of the C&AG, who can work only on the basis of annual reports prepared by Government departments or agencies. Therefore, it is a reactive look-back approach to accountability, which means we are really engaged in fretting about a horse that bolted the stable a year or so before.

At issue in that January 2003 meeting was the extraordinary divergence between the tax forecast for 2001 and the actual outturn. As the C&AG noted in his introduction to the report: 'Public spending was then based on an estimated tax take of €30.5 billion, whereas only €28 billion was received to fund that expenditure. One does not have to be a top flight accountant or economist to recognise that it would not be long before this scale of imbalance undermined the sustainability of budgetary decisions.' Tom Considine, secretary general of the Department of Finance, outlined the reasons why there had been such a disastrous €2.5 billion overestimation of tax revenues for the year, referring to the attacks of 11 September 2001 and the global economic downturn that followed. I was first up to examine Mr Considine.

> Every business in the country would have had predictions and would have suffered because of 11th of September but if they were to report a shortfall of €2.5 billion they would probably be out of business. That inaccuracy in their business predictions would not be acceptable. The question of public confidence arises due to this shortfall and particularly so

because of the meeting we had last week with the health boards and the inaccuracies that came to light arising from their management systems. What steps is the Department taking to explain the position to the public? What changes are being made to management systems and their understanding of the economy here and the impact of the global economy on it? How will the figures for 2003 stack up? The monthly reports that are available would have given an indication of something clearly going wrong with our figures.

I would have assumed that world events would always have been factored into the equation. Events such as 11 September will always have an impact on us. I accept the explanations given but I still cannot understand how this situation came about. If one takes the percentages of the shortfall as a percentage of the estimate—it was down 28% for customs and 15% for excise—one would expect a degree of movement within the figures because of the nature of the tax base. To say that there was a movement of 28% without its having been partly predicted requires further comment, in spite of the explanation the Secretary General has given.

PAYE returns are largely predictable. I can understand the movement of the figures pertaining thereto in terms of economic growth or a downturn. However, a shortfall of €762 million is worrying given the predictable system of collection. Surely this indicates that the system of management that produces the final figures needs to be overhauled. It calls into question the understanding of where we are going economically, even after one considers what is happening in the world economy. I would like to hear more comment on the systems that generate these figures before asking further questions.

Despite the fact that the Department of Finance had been out by €50 million a week, the secretary general insisted to the committee that there were no plans to change the methodology for forecasting that had so wrong-footed the Government. He also referred to the fact that, while it was no great consolation, other countries were having difficulties with tax forecasting. To my mind this demonstrated a kind of complacency that can be hugely corrosive as obsolete systems remain in place and are defended just because that is what officials have become accustomed to. This can all be seen in the context of my earlier observations on the Department of Finance and its performance in the intervening period, which is now thankfully being addressed by the Minister for Finance, Brian Lenihan.

MEDICAL CARDS FIASCO

In March 2003, the PAC dealt with a serious issue that derived from a decision in December 2000 by Charlie McCreevy, the then Minister for Finance, to automatically extend the free medical card scheme to all citizens over 70 years of age, his having announced a trebling of income thresholds for eligibility over three years from 1999. The committee was presented with a report from the C&AG that showed the cost of the scheme had risen from the €19 million per annum estimated in the 2001 budget, to a staggering €51 million. The departments of Finance and Health had seriously underestimated the number of people in the State over 70 years of age. The budget measure announced by McCreevy was costed on the basis of the 39,000 extra people advised by officials to now be eligible for the free medical card. However, by 2002 a total of 83,000 had applied—more than double the original estimate.

As a result of all of this, the GPs and pharmacists now had a whip hand in negotiations on public health contracts because the measure had already been announced and they managed to win a deal to treble the rates payable for existing patients for new patients under the scheme. This caused the cost of the general medical service to increase 55 per cent from 2001 to 2002. It also emerged that there were more over-70s medical cards than there were citizens over 70 in the State because GPs were being paid for patients who had passed away or were no longer resident. This, of course, put a strain on the public finances and subsequently led to serious political repercussions when proposals were made to curtail the hugely costly scheme in Brian Lenihan's first hairshirt Budget in 2008. The righteous indignation of the people over 70, who had made no error or mistaken calculation, caused a Government U-turn and the proposals to limit the scheme were dropped. It was a serious political miscalculation, about which I went on record, on the Sue Nunn programme on KCLR radio, saying that the 'two Brians' had 'made a bags of it'.

OFFICE OF PUBLIC WORKS

The systems, practices and control of the Office of Public Works, about which I had such concern, were subjected to considerable scrutiny before a meeting of the PAC in April 2003. The meeting was considering the C&AG's value for money report on the activities of the building maintenance service of the OPW. Its financial returns for 2000 showed it had managed to lose a staggering €4.3 million out of an expenditure of €11.3 million.

According to the report, the OPW had not included charges for all items due or had not invoiced for work at all because of a lack of a computer system, which caused me to wonder where the impress system they had told me about had gone and what was the state of their manual system across all their services.

I think the leasing of a site in Kilkenny is a good example of how careful the State is with your money.

In March 2002, the OPW leased a site at Leggetsrath, Kilkenny at a monthly rent of €15,322 with a pull-out clause if the project could not proceed. The site was leased so that the system-built accommodation to house 250 asylum-seekers could be constructed on it.

On 11 March 2002, the Minister made an order permitting the dispensing with of the requirement to obtain planning permission for the project. Within three days, on 14 March, a letter was sent to the tendering contractor by the OPW agreeing to the price of €6.56 million for the construction of the system. No 'subject to planning permission' clause was included, which, for a number of reasons, I think was ridiculous.

The OPW knew that solicitors representing the tenants were challenging the Minister regarding dispensation orders made in relation to Broc House in Donnybrook, Dublin and Lynch's Lodge in Macroom. Judicial reviews were pending on both these cases as a result of applications made in 2000. There was a reasonable probability that the orders would be revoked.

Kilkenny already had a home for asylum-seekers, which was in operation with the agreement and assistance of local people, and could provide future accommodation.

Local residents were up in arms and political pressure was being brought to bear in the Dáil.

The site was unsuitable. Indeed the local authority had told the OPW that they would not give planning permission because it was unserviced, at the back of residential houses and beside a railway track and, therefore, very unsuitable.

On 9 May 2002, the Attorney General directed that the OPW should not use Exemption Orders in any further cases without his permission!

The project at Leggetsrath could not proceed, but that did not mean the State stopped paying. The contractor was paid €2 million to compensate him for his costs. Rent at €15,322 per month continued to be paid for some time. Storage, insurance, etc. on prefabs and equipment costing €2 million continued to be paid until, I was later told in response to a PQ, they were handed to the army.

Including professional costs, the total cost of this debacle to the citizen of Ireland up to August 2003 was €2.5 million, without taking into account the money spent purchasing the prefabs and equipment.

Sean Benton said that the OPW was operating under instructions from the Department of Justice, Equality and Law Reform, whose advice from the Attorney General might conflict with the view of the local authority. But that did not explain away the fact that judicial reviews were pending, requiring all parties involved to be cautious. Neither did it, in my opinion, explain the fact that a contract had been signed, despite this, without a get-out clause. His claim that the OPW was acting as an agent had all the force of a Minister saying he acted on 'best advice', giving rise to the question: what about common sense and what about the very public presentation of strong arguments against anyone taking any action until the smoke had cleared? What was certain, however, was that no heads would be lost: just €2.5 million of public money.

Around this time, people were dying in hospital corridors, schools needed refurbishing and State systems needed to be modernised. The roar of the Celtic tiger drowned it all out, but it doesn't now. Too late.

CITY OF DUBLIN VEC

In July 2003, the C&AG drew the PAC's attention to a report on the City of Dublin Vocational Education Committee's accounts for 1998–2000. The audit revealed serious shortcomings in the VEC's accounting procedures and internal controls for managing its finances. A large part of the problem stemmed from difficulties in changing over to a new financial and accounting system, which was compounded by a high staff turnover. Consequently, essential control tasks were not being carried out. There were also weaknesses in reviewing and dealing with balances on self-financing projects, such as community employment schemes, and matters such as verifying the considerable petty cash balances held. Over the years there had not been any internal audit function in the largest VEC in the country.

Historically, this had been a weakness generally in the VEC sector but the Department of Education had moved to address the issue by setting up a support services unit to provide audit services for VECs. For some reason the mandate of the new unit did not extend to the City of Dublin Vocational Education Committee. The result was that the accounting firm that had been hired to audit the accounts had to resign from the job because there were insufficient records and it could not stand over or sign off on the accounts of a State organisation with a budget of nearly €90 million, which employs more than 3,500 people.

The CEO of the VEC, William Arundel, told the committee that the internal accounting systems had failed because of a high rate of staff turnover and the illness of the finance officer at the time. During the period, the VEC was engaged in a changeover to a computerised system for the reconciliation of accounts, the training for which, at nearly €90,000, ended up costing almost three times what had been first indicated.

Computers are often blamed by departments. A central purchasing and training section for ICT, staffed by specialists and accountants, could have saved the country a fortune and would have revealed, I am sure, huge deficiencies in their manual systems. These deficiencies inevitably, on a rubbish-in rubbish-out basis, cause further problems when computerised.

I pointed out that had a private business failed to account for its income and expenditure in the way the VEC had, it would be pursued by the Revenue Commissioners, Companies Office and others and would probably go out of business. I also underlined the fact that, despite the Department of Education and Science being made aware of the problems in the CDVEC for a number of years, they failed to resolve the problems that had been encountered, leading to the audit of the accounts being suspended twice. There seemed to be a complete lack of urgency about this disastrous situation.

TRIBUNALS

During my time as vice-chairman of the committee, the cost of the various tribunals of inquiry being conducted by the State was raised as an issue time and time again. I and my colleagues on the committee shared a growing public concern that some were dragging on, costing the taxpayer a fortune and with no end in sight. In November 2003, I and others asked the clerk of the PAC to write to the departments of the Taoiseach; Justice, Equality and Law Reform; and Environment, Heritage and Local Government and others to establish exactly what we were paying for these tribunals and what procedures were in place to monitor these costs.

The result of these inquiries was shocking. The Mahon (formerly Flood) Tribunal into certain planning matters was running at more than €30 million; the Moriarty Tribunal into certain payments to Charles Haughey and Michael Lowry had, to that point, cost €15.5 million; the Barron Inquiry into the Dublin and Monaghan bombings, €2.7 million; the Morris Tribunal, €9.2 million; the Barr Tribunal, €1.5 million. It also emerged that the vast majority of this money was being spent on lawyers commanding fees of €2,500 and €2,000 per day respectively for some senior and junior counsel and that, in many cases, the concluding dates and, therefore, the final cost of the inquiries could not be predicted.

The real problem, it seemed to me, was that the legal fees of witnesses called before the various tribunals would have to be covered by the State in most cases since most will be found blameless for any wrongdoing after being investigated. The various departments under whose aegis the inquiries were being conducted were completely unable to accurately predict the final bill in most cases. It was, and remains, a ticking financial time bomb.

The tribunals also need to be examined from a value-for-money perspective. There was and is an argument that, particularly in the case of Moriarty and Mahon, they will have paid for themselves in terms of tax revenue found to be owing. This is not good enough because the Criminal Assets Bureau would probably be more effective and efficient in collecting any monies due. Many people now view the tribunals as a wealth distribution system designed to move public money into the pockets of the legal profession, using a sad line of discredited individuals as a conduit. They also wonder if any of those under investigation will still be alive to be brought before the courts by the time some tribunals conclude.

In November 2003, having reviewed the information from the PAC's investigations, I made a statement in which I called for the tribunals to be wound down as soon as possible. I also pointed out that any such move would get broad public support because there was only so much venality and graft that people could take before turning away. The country cannot confidently move forward while so much of our moral energy and financial resources are being spent, however justifiably and under-standably, raking over the contaminated ashes of our cowboy past. At the time, I called for the Government to consider other, more cost-effective and efficient tribunal models and increase the powers of Dáil committees, like the PAC, to investigate and question in order to bring authority and responsibility back where it belongs. The Commissions of Investigations Act that followed in 2004 goes some way to addressing the issues raised then, but not quite far enough.

A NEW ACCOUNTABILITY?

Accountability and transparency are overused terms but they are vital to the trust that must exist between the Government and the governed. And nowhere is this more important than in the over-sight of the spending of money raised by taxing those citizens. On a day-to-day basis, the Dáil and Seanad can provide a forum for questioning public expenditure but their scope is limited. For serious and major issues, a commission of investigation or tribunal can be constituted but the gap between these forums needs to be bridged. Following the success of the DIRT inquiry, Oireachtas committees generally adopted a more investigative approach until the Supreme Court ruled to restrict such inquiries in the Maguire *v* Ardagh case on the Oireachtas sub-committee investigating the shooting of John Carthy in Abbeylara in 2000.

The subsequent interpretation of the Supreme Court's decision has been too restrictive, since such investigative powers are compatible with the Constitution. Elected representatives, such as those on the PAC, should be empowered to investigate and establish facts on their own initiative.

One of the main shortcomings of the PAC, however, is the long delay between the identification of serious issues by the C&AG, and their examination at meetings of the committee. If this State is to build trust with citizens it must provide political accountability and ensure value for money. The PAC needs to be able to deal with such controversies in real time rather than through the current look-back situation otherwise it will appear to be all sound and fury with no real teeth. Furthermore, policy decisions of ministers are not subject to scrutiny or questioning in any way and the committee cannot make any comment or recommendations in this regard.

Typically, following a PAC meeting at which officials endure a bruising encounter with the members, promises of reform and the introduction of better financial management are made but reform and change are very slow to happen and the committee can become involved again only when another problem has to be brought to its attention. During my time there, we instituted a practice that copied the minutes of the meetings, noting particular issues, to the Minister for Finance, asking him to respond to them directly to the people involved.

Nonetheless, I realised that while our role was very important, for the committee to have any real, genuine impact on the shocking waste, inefficiency and corruption that we discovered in the management of public money we needed to increase the committee's powers and scope to really make a difference. To that end, I helped prepare a report with Pat Rabbitte, who had been high-profile member of the committee and played a major role as vice-chairman of the DIRT inquiry. The document, once produced, typically rested on a shelf gathering dust.

A DIFFERENCE OF OPINION

Shortly before the Fianna Fáil Ard Fheis in Killarney in October 2005, I was asked by the Taoiseach, Bertie Ahern, to come up to his office following the Order of Business in the Dáil. I had made various public comments on national and local radio and in newspaper interviews to the effect that I believed the PAC needed to be significantly beefed up in terms of its scope and powers. When I arrived at the Taoiseach's office, the then Minister for Finance, Brian Cowen, was sitting there. I was asked what my problem was with the PAC and I outlined my case as clearly and carefully as possible. I said I was asking for the compellability of witnesses not employed by the State, the ability to examine current issues rather than operate on a look-back basis, and the ability to make recommendations for how public money could be better safeguarded and for sanctions against those who had failed to do so. I also asked that local government should come under the scrutiny of the C&AG and the committee.

Bertie Ahern sat back and listened as I outlined my proposals. As usual, it was hard to know what he was thinking. Not so with Brian Cowen—his position was clear and he was extraordinarily angry. I found myself on the receiving end of a tirade that, loud and blue, lasted for some time.

If he thought he was going to intimidate me he was wrong: I was not frightened. But I was interested. Not in what he had to say—the message was simple and plain enough—but in the fact that he had worked himself into a frenzy to say it.

Most messages of this nature are delivered by politicians

deliberately and coldly and some thought would have gone into them. Cowen was substituting tough for talk. Anger is driven by fear and insecurity. What was going on? He told me I should leave well enough alone and that he would not hear of any changes to the PAC. He was extremely agitated and I suspected that senior civil servants who had been challenged by me at PAC meetings had asked him to back them up and he, it seemed, was obliging.

The cause of the anger, I concluded, was the conflict between Cowen's legal and political brain, which I am sure could see the need for action, and the man who didn't want to rock the boat—and still doesn't—at any cost. It was not his job to oblige his officials or attempt, unsuccessfully, to bully me. He was Minister for Finance and the PAC was demonstrating that we had a public service, at senior level, that was Corinthian in both meanings of that word: amateur and profligate and, perhaps, something much worse. His job was to do something about it. Shooting the messenger wasn't what was required.

Put simply: this clever and experienced politician was a creature of his Department. He was doing what he had been told to do, despite the evidence now pouring out of the PAC that there was something wrong with the fundamental control and governance of the State. Cowen defended the status quo then and, despite the evidence provided by FÁS and other State delinquents, continues to do so now, at a time when real change is needed. Instead, we get doubtful compromises dressed as action, which will do no good.

I understand there is a need for caution with new and big decisions, but it is a cause for worry if the decisions are always cautious. That is why there must always be a distance between politicians and officials at all levels: it prevents the thinking of one dominating the other, to the detriment of both. Too many politicians over the past decade or so took doubtful 'best advice' rather than brave decisions. That is a big reason we are where we are today.

I turned to Brian Cowen as I was about to leave the room and I said:

> This cannot go on, there has to be change, too much money is being lost and we are losing the trust of the people. And another thing, Brian, next Saturday, thousands of fishermen will protest at the Fianna Fáil ard fheis seeking a ban on drift net fishing. I will be there with them, because they are right and we must act.

Still angry, he threw his hands in the air and his eyes to Heaven. I threw any belief I had in his ability to deliver change into the dustbin. Bertie had not said a word during the meeting. He just sat back and enjoyed the exchange.

Yet, some time later, because I believe we can all change and improve and that the conferring of power, and the responsibility it brings, can sometimes encourage people towards radical changes in character and attitude, I would have voted for Brian Cowen as leader of Fianna Fáil and Taoiseach. I wouldn't now.

Brian Cowen's reaction to my proposals on the PAC that afternoon is, to some extent, a microcosm of my relationship with the leadership of the party in Government. With a background in business and experience of many, many years solving the problems encountered by people in their interactions with the State, my impatience for change and reform have led me into conflict.

Chapter 9 ∿

A FAILURE OF ENTERPRISE

Following the general election of 24 May 2007, Bertie Ahern was again elected Taoiseach by the new Dáil on 14 June. The Progressive Democrats had lost four of their six seats in the election, two of which had been held by junior ministers. An agreement was reached between Fianna Fáil and the Green Party to increase the number of ministers of state from 17 to 20. This gave Ahern the opportunity to introduce a new team of juniors to Government and he usually chose TDs who had served some time in the Dáil.

Carlow-Kilkenny had again delivered three out of five seats for Fianna Fáil and Mary White had taken a seat for the Green Party, bringing the Government tally to four. I was a TD with 10 years' experience who had played an active role in two Dáil committees, so I hoped I might get a call.

Bertie Ahern rang me on Tuesday, 19 June 2007, and asked me to come to Leinster House early the following morning. When I got there, I found that Brendan Smith, Máire Hoctor, Jimmy Devins, Pat Carey, Billy Kelleher, Michael Kitt and Trevor Sargent were all waiting to meet the Taoiseach.

Bertie Ahern is an enigma. Everyone knows who he is but only a very few really know him, and they aren't his party colleagues. He is a master of the tight embrace, the hearty laugh and light banter: 'Howaya, John? How are the Cats? That Cody is a fierce man altogether. You're doing well,' etc. etc. You don't get near the private person or his thought processes but that is a useful skill for a politician and a leader to have. He wasn't afraid to give it to you between the eyes, short and sharp, but you would still get a clap on the back as you were leaving, maybe to remind you it could have been a knife.

He was a pragmatic compromiser, a deal maker and a very skilled politician. His claim that he was a socialist didn't mean he was in Joe Higgins's gang. But it was not without foundation and I always found him to be sympathetic, and when I wanted action on social issues, I usually got it. Also, as leader of Fianna Fáil, he considered the organisation's many voluntary workers and always made sure that their work was acknowledged.

His 'dig outs' got him into trouble and brought him down but, long after they are forgotten, his contribution to the peace in Northern Ireland, when he shook hands that many would not touch and where his negotiating skills and his pragmatism came to the fore, will be remembered. Undoubtedly, he helped save thousands of lives.

He was his usual self when my turn came to go into his office. We exchanged pleasantries and he told me I was getting the trade and commerce portfolio in the Department of Enterprise, Trade and Employment. This was arguably the most significant of the posts being filled, because responsibility for trade and commerce is a delegated Cabinet function. Indeed, in many countries the holder of the trade and commerce portfolio is a full Cabinet Minister.

The Taoiseach told me he expected a great deal from me because of the central importance of the Department to the economy, which was already showing signs of stalling. He said he wanted to see me driving an agenda that would help grow the economy. I thanked him for his confidence in me and assured him I would do my best.

I was delighted with the appointment. It was obviously a great honour for me and my family, and my supporters and people in the constituency would be pleased. For me, politics is a vocation not a career path, but that didn't mean I didn't want or welcome promotion, which gave me the opportunity to use my experience and what skills I had to best purpose. It was an opportunity to make a difference and an exciting challenge. I didn't realise then just how difficult a challenge it would prove to be.

I left the Taoiseach's office in high spirits. As I walked into the long corridor, I passed a group of secretaries general of various departments coming out of a meeting. Among them was Sean Benton from the Office of Public Works. 'Don't worry, Sean—I didn't get the OPW,' I told him. You have to spread happiness around.

I know that the general perception of ministers, both junior and senior, in the public mind and, to a surprising extent, in the media, is of someone who runs a Department and makes things happen. That might have been the case in Lemass's time, but it is not true now to any great extent. Quite often, a Minister is someone run by the Department, to whom, at the whim of the Department, things happen. You can choose the path of accepting the Department's warm embrace and take the best advice of officials, who will provide your speeches, give you your photo opportunities and good press events and generally treat you like a cuddly toy mascot. Or you can, maybe with their assistance, begin to drive your party's political agenda. In short, you can become a nodding head on the back window of the departmental machine or an annoyance hanging off its rearview mirror where they hope they can keep an eye on you.

The latter requires you to know and understand your brief and have the confidence and energy to go against the tide of departmental disapproval. That was the path I would take. But that was the future. Now I was on my way to my Department.

The headquarters of what is now the Department of Enterprise, Trade and Innovation are on Kildare Street, just across from Leinster House and the rear of Government Buildings. The austere grey art deco building was designed by J.R. Boyd Barrett (a grand-uncle of People Before Profit councillor Richard Boyd

Barrett) and is decorated with relief sculptures by Gabriel Hayes, which depict Brendan the Navigator and heroic Irish mythical figures bringing divine energy to the industry of the country. One of the original departments of state established by the First Dáil in 1919, the Department of Trade and Commerce under Ernest Blythe soon became the Department of Industry and Commerce, coaxing a shattered economy into life and nurturing it for the country's citizens. I think Brendan's navigation may have let him down sometime around 2001.

By the time Sean Lemass was elected Taoiseach in 1959, he had served as Minister for Industry and Commerce for nearly 20 years through four administrations in the 1930s, 40s and 50s. Subsequent taoisigh who served as ministers in the Department, which has had no less than eight name changes since 1977, include Jack Lynch, Garret FitzGerald, John Bruton, Albert Reynolds and Bertie Ahern, reflecting its central role in Government and its vital influence on the development and growth of the Irish economy since Independence.

The list of names alone illustrates the changing nature of ministerial appointments and provides an understandable reason for the Civil Service's belief in its indestructibility and independence and, perhaps, its inclination to view ministers as political bubbles on its going on forever stream. That can be resolved by leaving ministers in their departments for longer. The modern tendency is to change ministers often, demonstrating two negative views: ministers are simply strong political faces who don't need to know their departments and civil servants are in control. It wasn't surprising, therefore, that none of the departments of the newly appointed junior ministers were setting off fireworks to celebrate our arrival. On the other hand, it would have been courteous and possibly diplomatic for the secretary general of my new Department to have called me on my mobile to say hello, offer congratulations and arrange a briefing meeting. It didn't happen. The champagne wasn't being cooled?

I walked into the Department without any idea of where I had to go and what was to happen. So I went up and spoke to another Minister in the Department, Michael Ahern. I wasn't directed to an office and no one told me I had an office—come back Donal O'Brien, all is forgiven. Michael suggested that I take an empty room beside him and I went there—immediate demotion: Minister to squatter.

I now had a chair and a telephone and—somewhere—a Department, which clearly wasn't in a hurry to throw its arms around me. I began making a list: private secretary, staff, computer, furnishings. I was back in the Mayor's Room in Kilkenny in 1996 except there was nobody like Paddy Donnelly around.

Those first few days in that Department were seriously disturbing. I wondered, if this was what was happening to me, a Minister, albeit junior, in an Irish Government, and I don't care how grand that sounds, what the hell was happening to the people, businesses and organisations with which the Department was dealing on a daily basis? But I was really only at the beginning of an eye-opening and frustrating experience.

At this point, I have to emphasise that this was my experience. It may not have happened to others and it may have happened to me because my reputation preceded me and someone felt a bit of wing clipping and place-putting was in order. If that was the case, it was disrespectful to the office I held, bad mannered and totally misjudged.

I had a job to do and I didn't have an office and I hadn't got a briefing. In fact, I never got a briefing, all I got was a rule book regarding my responsibilities and duties as a Minister. Message sent: Ministers don't count. Message received: Time to stand up.

I needed to get a personal private secretary quickly and he or she had to come from the ranks of the Civil Service. That was fine with me, but I wanted someone with experience, whom I liked, not a minder foisted on me by the Department.

Eamonn McCormack was recommended and I met and liked

him. He had worked as a private secretary for Mary O'Rourke for years, on secondment from my Department, had buckets of experience and wanted the job. He had experience of setting up offices from scratch and he ran Mary's office when she was Leader of the Seanad. It should have been easy, but it wasn't.

It was now two or three weeks since my arrival and I was being treated like a hedgehog in a balloon factory by the Department. I went to see the human resources section, who had made no attempt to see me. First of all I was told I couldn't have Eamonn and it was clear they didn't want to give me Eamonn. When I insisted, I was told that there had to be an interview process. I more or less said don't talk nonsense, I know the man I want and there is probably nobody in the Civil Service with better qualifications for the job. Ah, no. The rule book, an interview had to take place. More time, more waste.

Two or three weeks later, I had to sit at what was, essentially, a charade, where Eamonn and two other much less experienced people were interviewed and marked. Guess what? Eamonn got the job. He was appointed on 20 July, a month after I became a Minister.

That's the problem with petty rules: they turn common sense on its head and upset your moral compass, which can lead you unwittingly into the distasteful game I had just played—I'm not saying I don't sin, but I don't like being led into it. The fact was that I had been put in the position of being insincere to two people. It is completely false, a lot of this politically correct stuff, and it offends.

My experience of the first few weeks and months in the Department were a disturbing and depressing reflection of what was also being experienced by businesses, trade organisations and representative bodies. Again, this is a comment not so much on the many public servants who do excellent work in the Department but rather of the system that is calibrated so as to put the brakes on anything that progresses faster than the standard speed dictated, in many cases, by the public sector unions. This system of administration, bound by the parameters of work practices agreed between the unions and the Government has, in the Department of Enterprise, Trade and Employment—as with many other departments—created speed bumps and barriers to real reform. The irony is that those who most resist reform of work practices and greater flexibility are the very people who would benefit most from it.

About two months after my appointment, I now had a private secretary and he found two Civil Service staff, who learned to live with the fun we were having and were a great help with the workload in the Dublin office. My appointment had added an extra Junior Minister to the Department and we were still without a proper office, although the Department, during the Dáil recess, was now going to renovate the space I was squatting in.

I must have been in the Department at least three weeks before I met the secretary general, Sean Gorman. But I never got a briefing or the feeling that what I was doing was worthwhile.

Meanwhile, the two staff I had in Kilkenny, a very busy and efficient constituency office, were inundated with the extra work that was coming in because I was a Minister. I was entitled to two support staff from the Department so I asked to have a person assigned to me, with experience of dealing with policy and legislative work. But I was told, after four weeks, that no such person was available and I should hire one myself. The Department told me to approach a recruitment agency to get the position filled. A suitable person was found, Lorraine Shelley, and I had to pay her myself while waiting for the Department to put her on the books. Then, another problem.

I was informed by the head of my Department's human resources section that the Department of Finance had not approved the appointment. Another fight began while I continued to pay her out of my own pocket. I brought the matter up with Sean Gorman, and pointed out that his Department had sanctioned my action. Ah, yes, but the Department of Finance had not. He didn't seem too bothered. After all, I was only the Minister for Trade and Commerce and half the business community wanted to speak to me, book appointments, seek assistance and make complaints about the Department I was working in. I decided to bother him.

I told the Department that I had employed Lorraine on their instructions and if I had to let her go I would be a willing witness in her action for breach of contract. The Department of Finance sought legal advice from the Attorney General about Lorraine's employment! Suddenly, blue sky. It was amazing how fast they could act when they wanted to. Her appointment was confirmed on 9 November, nearly five months after I had entered the Department.

As I was losing time and energy shaking nickels and dimes out of a Department wasting time and money, my constituency work, my parliamentary work and my ministerial work was piling up, because, in my opinion, the people in charge simply had no understanding of urgency and were largely floating above, particularly, the growing turmoil in the SME sector. Don't believe me? Ask the SME sector.

While all of this nonsense was going on, I had to speak in the Dáil, attend meetings in Europe and the Department and fulfil appointments throughout the country. I was enjoying the work but was getting really tired of the frustrations and, frankly, worried about the quality and commitment of senior management within the Department.

In an attempt to improve my own time management I hired, and paid for myself, an IT specialist who was a friend of my son's. He discovered that more officials than I believed was necessary or desirable were accessing my diary, including people I believed had no need to know. I wasn't comfortable with that and I decided to stop it as part of organising my online diary system.

Again, this was not preciousness on my part, it was about

restoring respect for the office. There seemed to be something wrong with the pecking order as far as information was concerned. Senior civil servants could access my diary to see who I was meeting and where I was going. I couldn't access theirs! I have no objection in principle to the transparency of my work, but only to senior civil servants who are prepared to be transparent about what they are doing.

I installed a new, more efficient system, which linked me, my office in the Department and my constituency office together, limiting outside access to my private secretary, Eamonn McCormack, with whom officials in the Department would have to communicate. For me, this was about taking charge of my Department. I did not think it was unreasonable that officials reporting to me should be required to go through my secretary or knock on my door, which was always open.

The Department, of course, liked none of this. It was now unable to intervene in my arrangements and meetings without talking to me or being told by me. Furthermore, I was establishing precedents that could trouble it in the future. But the alternative was an acknowledgment by me that I did not have control.

Concerned about the amount of time I was spending on mind-boggling internal departmental politics—when did these people have time to do anything else?—and in order to avoid the delays that had dogged the appointment of my office's staff in the first few months, I decided to hire in, and pay for myself, a private company to train Eamonn in Dublin and Lorraine in Kilkenny how to use the system and, in turn, they trained the other staff members as necessary. It was only common sense that my departmental office would be compatible with my constituency office, which is, for a TD's operation, relatively technologically advanced. It's not quite state-of-the-art but we have efficient IT systems for tracking constituents' cases, parliamentary questions and correspondence with the myriad agencies and offices that deliver public services.

Common sense didn't work. My approach to synchronising the IT capabilities of my departmental office and my constituency office had caused problems in the Department! I was informed that my system could not be supported by the Department because it was too advanced! Bizarrely, the Department had to agree to allow the Oireachtas to continue supporting my constituency system as they had the technical resources to do so.

I want to remind you again, citizen, that this was a Department at the cutting edge of Ireland's attempt to sell itself to the world— I was later to recommend, with no success, that it equip itself with an interactive website. However, every senior manager had a Blackberry and there was a great deal of gossip regarding body language as a substitute for action from what I called my 'Blackberry bush'. I have no idea what it all cost. For example, I told the secretary general during a conversation that I was a nervous traveller—perhaps I have an inclination towards control! Within an hour, Micheál Martin, the then Minister for Enterprise, called. 'What do you mean you don't like travel?' he asked. Perplexed, I responded: 'I didn't say I wouldn't travel—who told you that?' He said: 'Sean Gorman said you won't travel.' To which I responded: 'I don't like travelling long-haul flights, Micheál, but that's not to say that I won't travel—I understand the job I have to do.' Baby talk in a serious world.

With those teething problems set aside, we managed to get going as an efficient operation. The Department had allocated another person to the Kilkenny office who was very pleasant but not nearly experienced or well-equipped enough to deal with the volume and nature of the enquiries that were coming in. If the time that was expended on dealing with the red tape and petty squabbles around setting up my office in the summer of 2007 was spent on dealing with the urgent enquiries of small businesses, exporters and others, we might have made more progress.

Making progress with the Green Party over the Control of Exports Bill wasn't easy either. The Greens had huge concerns about the sale of weapons and anything even remotely connected with instruments of torture or parts for same.

Now, if you consider the various eye-watering uses a simple mousetrap could be put to you will begin to understand my difficulty with dealing with this level of concern. I get the bill through the House after lengthy meetings with the representative of the Greens and their advisers, but not before every nut and bolt had been examined and decisions taken about how to control the possibility of ploughs being turned into swords.

Their concerns were exaggerated and silly. They were demanding measures that could not be put in the bill and looking for controls over private companies that would bury those companies under red tape and regulation, and would still be impossible to police.

Actually, I usually welcome the fact that the Greens have a say, but they can be naïve and obsessive with their single-issue stands. Precariously balanced between extinction and distinction, they are inclined, when they get their hands on a lever of power, to push it to the floor, at the risk of blowing up the engine. All well and good and sometimes admirable, but we do have a country to run, waste-treatment plants to build and, almost certainly, nuclear power to consider.

I didn't find it hard to understand the culture of a Department dealing with trade and commerce. I found it impossible. Senior managers were simply not up to speed and the Minister, Mary Coughlan, wasn't either. I'm a politician and actually we are a tolerant and humane profession, whatever you might believe, and we don't like to stray into the black and white, but this was spaceship territory. I saw how hard it was out there to make a shilling and the economic environment was getting worse. I can understand if you are reading this with disbelief but what I am telling you is the truth. It was enormously frustrating.

I know that a business approach annoys some people who associate it with a lack of humanity and a hard-hearted, uncaring obsession with making money: knowing the price of everything and the worth of nothing. That is sometimes true or partly true but it is not what I mean. More often than not business is about creativity within the frame of the balance sheet, an opportunity to face challenges and pursue excellence and self-development. Making a profit is for many not just a desire for success but an objective measure of how well you are doing.

As a politician who was a small businessman, I understand the value of that approach. In the public service I believe the profit we should work for is the happiness and public satisfaction delivered, as with business, within a frame of cost control, the pursuit of excellence and the achievement of personal goals by motivated staff.

There were set pieces and set ways of going about the business of the Department. There was no immediate response to the needs of businesses and, to my mind no great understanding of how to create an environment where businesses could grow and prosper, or even establish themselves. There was no under-standing of the difficulties that businesses were beginning to face at that time and there was absolutely no policy to deal with the emerging crisis in the economy.

A very good example of this lack of response and under-standing is the way the Department treated the county enterprise boards. Their representative body had written to the Department on a number of occasions over a year or more regarding changes that would make the grant system more efficient and effective. This was important and necessary and should have been dealt with without delay. It wasn't dealt with at all. They didn't even get an acknowledgment.

The boards approached me after I was appointed, as I was the Minister responsible, complaining about the lack of response. I questioned the section involved without any success. I was met with indifference, and forceful language at one meeting didn't make any impact either. At one stage I felt it necessary to remind those present that I was the Minister and not a junior member of their staff, and I would make the decisions. All to no avail.

After a number of months, I raised the matter again only to find that the section had decided to bypass me by taking the matter up with Mary Coughlan. She and the section then did nothing because, up to the time I left, the enterprise boards were telling me that nothing was being done.

It was a divide and conquer tactic that worked because of the lack of a united political front. But it was the country that suffered, and also my relationship with my Minister and some senior civil servants.

Like most departments, the day-to-day management and the longer-term strategy of Enterprise, Trade and Employment was discussed at meetings of the Management Advisory Committee—called MACS—which would involve the Minister, junior ministers and senior civil servants. In my experience, these meetings were fairly pointless talking shops that were undertaken to tick some box on a management-system form. They were usually inconclusive, rarely arrived at any decisions and hardly ever resulted in any actual action being taken.

At a particular budget meeting in 2008, to give just one example, I had signalled in advance a proposal to eliminate the need to cut funding to the county enterprise boards by finding specific savings elsewhere in the Department's administration budget. At a time when small business needed to be supported most, I felt we could not afford to cut back on the vital supports delivered through the enterprise boards.

Minister Mary Coughlan and Junior Minister Billy Kelleher were at the meeting and we worked through the agenda until we reached my proposal, at which point my two fellow ministers departed and I was left to get down to the nitty-gritty with the accounting officer and the assistant secretary. Unsurprisingly, with the tacit political cover provided by the withdrawal of my colleagues, my proposals were rejected and funding to the county enterprise boards was cut—a decision I'm afraid we will live to regret.

So concerned was I about this response that I wrote to the assistant secretary of the Department, Gerry Donnelly, copied to Mary Coughlan, asking that 'the management of the city and county enterprise boards be vested in Shannon. Value for money and efficiency should be achieved by the Shannon unit and monthly reports should be made available to me as Minister responsible for the CEBS.'

The system in the Department and in the Civil Service as a whole is largely driven, if that is the word, by senior civil servants. But below that level there are many willing and able people that a hierarchical system prevents from making the contribution they are capable of. The system completely fails to motivate and enthuse young civil servants or provide forums where they can propose ideas for improving how they work or what they can deliver to the public. I personally know of dozens, but I suspect there are many thousands, of bright, eager people who enter the Civil Service with great intentions only to find themselves sucked into a machine that slowly grinds out of them, or suppresses, their initiative, innovation and passion.

Regardless of which ministers are at the helm, the ships of State are crewed by the same civil servants whose job it is to deliver government and public services to the citizens. For any Minister to be successful in pursuing real change and reform and a policy agenda that has been mandated by the people, the bureaucratic structure in those departments needs to be overhauled. It is difficult for a reforming Minister or one who is interested in some level of reform to actually achieve it in a Department that is stuck in a different age. The Department of Enterprise, Trade and Employment was and is heavily bureaucratic and unionised. I have no problem with unions in principle but they need to adapt and learn to be flexible in order to best protect the interests of their members in the long term.

Let's not fool ourselves. There is nothing about the, renamed, Department of Enterprise, Trade and Innovation that lives up to its title. It has within it the brains and ability, but not the culture or the drive. Its senior management should be ashamed of its performance, but not so ashamed that they will dredge up a defence.

NATIONAL STANDARDS AUTHORITY

One of the ideas I sought to implement while a Minister was the application of a National Standards Authority of Ireland (NSAI) code to the work of each and every Government Department and agency so that the public could have confidence that the State's system of governance was meeting the standards that would be expected at the highest level in the private sector. My thinking was that if the Government could set the bar high for itself, it would encourage others to reach it. These externally set criteria would also have the effect of measuring and, more importantly, valuing the work done by civil servants, giving them, at least, some degree of job satisfaction as well as providing taxpayers with a better service.

I met with the chief executive and the board of the NSAI, an agency for which I have the greatest respect, about drawing up a set of standards, similar to ISO 9000s—which we were encouraging every company in the country to attain—tailored to meet the specific requirements of any Government Department. They responded very positively and we made some good progress in developing a cost-effective standard. I decided that the Department of Enterprise, Trade and Employment would be the lead Department in the initiative, even if it was only piloted in those areas where we interfaced with the public. I spoke to the secretary general, Sean Gorman, about the plan. He appeared unimpressed and obviously reluctant to subject the Department to the degree of scrutiny necessary to measure and apply such a standard.

It was pretty depressing. On one hand, I'm kicking against the Department's inertia and on the other I'm running around the world telling investors they can rely on what I know is a totally incompetent State Department. I banged on about it with the secretary general and he kicked for touch, with a precision that Ronan O'Gara would envy. Paddy Donnelly, where are you?

I continued to pursue the matter with the secretary general who, in the end, gave me a commitment that he would examine the possibility of introducing the standard. I heard nothing further from him in relation to the project. But I am sure that by this time I was becoming a project for him.

The Department's argument was that it had its own standards, which were measured against the strategic management initiative within which certain goals are met. However, none of those relate at all to how a Department should function in its delivery of services to the public. It is effectively an in-house form-filling exercise designed to confuse and has little to do with genuine productivity when benchmarked against any standards in the business world related to productivity. Remember the Department of Finance's Annual Output Statement, which I covered earlier and what I said about internal auditing? Generally, internal reports from the public service should be treated with petrol and a match.

The NSAI is an example of how a State agency should be run. It applies the highest standards to itself in developing standards for others and actually operates at a profit to the Exchequer. The work on the ISO 9000 standard for Government departments and agencies has been done and could be implemented in short order if the political will existed to do so. Sadly, I don't believe that political will is there at the time of writing.

FORAS ÁISEANNA SAOTHAIR—FÁS

During the early part of 2008 in the course of my work with officials in the Department, other agencies and business people, I began to hear of serious concerns about the conduct of the State training agency Foras Áiseanna Saothair, an institution about which I already had my doubts. Known to all as FÁS, the agency was established during Ireland's last serious recession in 1988 with the purpose of giving assistance to those seeking employment by providing training, apprenticeships, job placements and advice to unemployed citizens. By 2008 its budget had grown to around €1 billion, an extraordinary sum for an agency that, during the years of the boom, was operating in an economy that had effectively enjoyed full employment.

In May 2008, on foot of an internal audit report produced by FÁS more than a year earlier that raised more questions than it answered, the C&AG published a report on a series of irregularities in the handling of the agency's advertising budget. The C&AG's report detailed a litany of failures to achieve value for money with €1.7 million being spent on a website that duplicated the work of an existing site and €160,000 in incorrect payments made to media outlets that had added percentages to their invoices. Although the report was specific to the particular issue of the agency's advertising budget, it was clear the surface had just been scratched.

Increasingly concerned about what was being slowly revealed, on 10 September 2008 I wrote to Gerry Donnelly, the assistant secretary of the Department of Enterprise, Trade and Employment, copying the Tánaiste, asking for a full independent external audit and inquiry into FÁS's governance and financial affairs. I felt that such a comprehensive and transparent inquiry would demonstrate to the business community that we were serious about demanding the best of our public service and had intent with regard to the reform of FÁS. I imagine at this stage, you are probably not surprised that I did not receive any reply to this letter.

Subsequently, the Tánaiste did ask the C&AG to initiate another inquiry into FÁS but he was keen to hold off until the conclusion of hearings of the Public Accounts Committee regarding his first report. The PAC meetings in October and November 2008, which first heard from FÁS director general Rody Molloy, had to be

suspended because of a failure by the agency to provide documents requested by the committee. On 23 November, the *Sunday
Independent* published an investigative article by Shane Ross and
Nick Webb that showed how FÁS executives had splashed
€643,000 in foreign trips over four years, including expenses on
four-star hotels, gourmet meals, beauty treatments and first-class
airfares. The following day, seemingly oblivious to the growing
public anger about the revelations, Rody Molloy, speaking on
'Today with Pat Kenny' on RTÉ Radio One, defended his practice
of exchanging one first-class airline ticket for two business-class
tickets so that his wife could travel with him. In fact, he claimed
he was 'entitled' to do so.

That day, I was at an event, presenting awards to young people
in White's Hotel in Wexford, when word of the interview came
through. The issue was raised at a meeting of the Fianna Fáil
parliamentary party the following evening and a number of TDs
and senators were furious as Brian Cowen had earlier backed
Rody Molloy, saying he had full confidence in him. At 11pm that
night the board of FÁS issued a statement to the effect that it had
accepted Molloy's resignation. The following day, the Opposition
piled the pressure on the Government to define and limit the
anticipated golden handshake that Molloy might get. The
Taoiseach replied that Molloy had acted honourably and with
accountability in his decision to resign and that his severance
package would be treated 'in accordance with public service
norms'.

Fast forward a year to September 2009. The C&AG published his
report on FÁS advertising expenditure, highlighting—among
other disgraceful wastes of spending—the creation of a television
advertisement for €600,000 that was never aired. Meanwhile,
as had been feared, it emerged that Rody Molloy had received a
€1.4 million pension top-up as the Tanaiste and the Minister for
Finance signed off on an increase in his service by five years from
55 to 60 as a sweetener following his resignation.

The secretary general of the Department of Enterprise, Trade and Employment, Sean Gorman, told the PAC that the pension top-up had been agreed because Rody Molloy had threatened legal action against the State if it did not accede to his demands for this golden handshake. It then emerged that no legal advice had been sought or given on Molloy's threat and the Minister and the Department had just caved in, although they denied the threat had been a deciding factor in the agreement. The Opposition again piled pressure on Mary Coughlan, calling on her to go, but Brian Cowen reaffirmed his full confidence in her.

MISSED OPPORTUNITY

Mary Coughlan was appointed by Brian Cowen as the new Minister for Enterprise in May 2008. I knew Mary quite well. She was a gregarious character, very sociable and much liked by her colleagues. She had come from the Department of Agriculture, where it was generally accepted that she had done a good job. However, she was now entering a field she was much less familiar with and it would prove to be very difficult for her. In addition, her style of management was hands-off and she was in a Department that needed a great deal of hands-on to encourage significant change in its methods. In hindsight, our two approaches were so different that we were bound to clash.

Towards the end of that year, as the financial crisis rocked the economic and social foundations of the country, she proposed at a meeting in the Department that we should have something akin to a 'war room' to deal with the emerging economic crisis and to which business people would be central. She said we could not continue with 'business as usual' and that if legislation was necessary it would be brought forward on an emergency basis in order to allow business to work, to allow the country to function and to generate the necessary tax revenue. I was enormously encouraged and a little surprised by her proposals, which, on the face of it, called for the action I was very keen to see taken. Indeed,

I complimented the Tánaiste on her initiatives, reflecting that, if this was going to be her approach in the Department, we had cause for hope. Sadly, the proposals remained promised and what we got was further drift. I think Mary was persuaded to fall in with the official Department line.

Early on in my time at the Department, I was asked by the management team of a global food processing giant to meet them to discuss their concerns over the regulation of CO_2 emissions and how they could best, and most cost-effectively, become fully compliant. At the meeting, the executives explained how they had developed a model for CO_2 emissions compliance, which while not in line with the Department's guidelines, was far more efficient and cost-effective and had the potential to act as a model for industry in Ireland and perhaps the rest of Europe. I was impressed by their proposal and, because of the huge numbers of employees involved and the significance of the sector to the economy, I requested senior figures in the Department to meet with the company and explore the whole matter in detail, reporting back to me.

A few months later, at a management meeting in the Department, I asked Sean Gorman what progress had been made. I was told the meeting had never taken place and, despite some officials' annoyance at my demanding progress reports, I was promised that a meeting would be arranged. But there was no urgency about it as far as I could see. I continued to press but made little progress. I am aware that, to date, the meeting still has not happened. Again, you have to take an auditing view on this. If this was what was happening to me, how many other companies out there were having their good ideas put in the Department's dustbin?

Among the literally hundreds of meetings I had with all types of stakeholders in the area under which my portfolio of trade and commerce fell, one was with the economist and writer David McWilliams, who proposed a very novel project that had been undertaken with great success in Argentina following that country's economic crisis. It is a website-based enterprise that involves what he described as a state-sponsored online match-making service to link young emerging companies with older experienced heads. I suggested to the Tanaiste that David McWilliams would act as an advisor and that an IT specialist would be appointed to fully gear up the Department's website and to create an interactive network for business people. Again, I received no response to that written request.

I discovered quickly that it is very difficult for a reforming Minister to work in an environment where some colleagues are stuck in another age, unionised, unmoving and lacking in flexibility. There was no drive or direction among the staff in the Department despite the fact that there were some very good, committed and hardworking people among them. The system managed to dampen down any enthusiasm for lateral thinking or innovation, which made it much easier to revert to the line of least resistance in all matters.

COMPANY LAW CONSOLIDATION BILL

One of the most pressing items on my agenda when I first came into the Department was a policy promise that we would bring together all the disparate company law legislation in one bill. It would be a huge document containing 1,300 sections, but it would update all the previous acts. Delivery had been promised for 2008, 2009 and 2010 but it was proceeding at a snail's pace and I was determined to make headway. And I was to discover that determination is not enough.

I met with a wide range of officials working on the bill to determine how complex it was and what progress was being made. With some officials I made no progress at all, my interest was as welcome as my suggestion that certain sections of the bill be farmed out and additional draughtsmen be taken on internally to move the work along. I was assured that everything was being done to bring speed to the process to ensure that the bill would be before the Dáil in the course of 2008 or 2009. I could not see that happening and I made various suggestions about how more speed could be introduced without any success.

As my frustration increased I sought the help of Labour TD Willie Penrose, chairman of the Committee on Enterprise and Small Business, to get his committee in to discuss and give their input on the bill. He kindly agreed to help, but I could not get the responsible section in the Department to agree to a meeting. Today the legislation remains stuck in the Department. Anyone waiting for the Companies Consolidation Bill should not hold their breath. Your need doesn't count any more than my determination.

DEPARTMENTAL LIFE

The clocks in the Department were set at leisurely. Hurry didn't happen and reality was something only the people fighting for survival in a weakening economy understood. At one stage, I was invited to a think-in in Druid's Glen—I began think-in about golf, which I don't play, and suggested that they think-in in the Department's meeting room. Despite this good advice they went to Druid's Glen. No report on the conclusions reached by the think-in ever crossed my desk, not even a score card.

There was only one difference between the meetings within the Department and the think-ins outside it: the expense was greater. The results were always the same. I'm no killjoy and I'm not against bonding sessions but only as a reward for progress, not inertia. Furthermore, I didn't want to become a member of a club that could weaken my determination. A healthy distance had to be maintained. I was fully aware that my attendance could be a mark of approval that bound me to the expense.

I had the same attitude to the credit card I was given. I did not approve and I didn't want the temptation in my pocket. And I didn't approve of the number of senior civil servants who had departmental credit cards. I wasn't going to join that club either. I sent it back.

I admit to my guard slipping a bit when I was asked at Christmas for €3,000 out of the personal ministerial piggy bank that I didn't know I had and never used. I was told it was for the staff Christmas party and other ministers had contributed. I thought, between all the ministers, that that was rather a lot of money for a Christmas party with an entrance fee. I discovered much later that the Department had declared it as a ministerial expense so press and public thought I had spent €3,000 on general expenses. They didn't get it the following Christmas. I refused point blank. I wonder how many other ministers had their expenses inflated in the same manner.

While credit cards were available and Christmas parties were being lavishly funded, it was difficult for me to even get the basic stationery for my office in Kilkenny. I was no longer supplied by the Dáil and the Department had no meaningful supply store in-house. Central procurement does not seem to have been in place in the Department of Enterprise.

In general, the spirit of enterprise and a can-do attitude just did not exist, resulting in very poor or no leadership for the country's business community. The exceptions to this were the IDA and Enterprise Ireland, which are outside agencies of the Department. Overall, the Department seemed to function more effectively for one side of the social partnership. Legislation and other considerations relative to the union agenda took priority.

It is very easy to slip into the culture, where a few actions, the consequences of which are not obvious and are not pointed out, can quickly make you a member of the club. Druid's Glen, credit cards, doubtful expenses descriptions and either observing or avoiding petty rules all take their toll.

My next experience wasn't petty. It was simply a power play, the second of its kind regarding my authority. As Minister for Trade and Commerce, I had the right to appoint some members of State boards—the other appointments came from professional bodies, etc. I was careful about this responsibility, appointing, in all, one politician, whose abilities I was confident about, and four professionals who have, I think, proven to be very suitable for the boards to which they were appointed.

The first appointment I had trouble with was one I made to the Irish Auditing and Accounting Supervisory Authority. On the day, three warrants arrived for me to sign, without comment. I was surprised, because I knew one of the appointments was mine. I checked the warrants and discovered that the selection had been made for me: my warrant was appointing an official of the Department! I rang the official and said I didn't approve of this and it wasn't going to happen. I do my own appointments. There was a bit of huffing and puffing and, extraordinarily, I was questioned about the qualifications of the candidate I was appointing, which were impeccable. I cut this conversation short and told the official I would appoint anyone I thought fit, gave the name and requested a revised warrant. My candidate was appointed.

The next appointment that caused difficulties was one I made to the NSAI, a body that I admire. I was told by the chairman that it would be really helpful if I could find someone experienced in medical devices to advise on standards. I found the research and development director of the Royal College of Surgeons. I didn't know him, and still don't, but obviously he was our man. Then the fun began.

I asked the Department to prepare a warrant. Nothing happened for so long that I told Eamonn to prepare one on the appropriate paper, which I would sign. When I told the Department I had my own warrant ready, an official informed me, with a great deal of self-satisfied tut-tutting, that it could not be sent out before the Taoiseach had been informed, so there. It was clear that this would not happen anytime soon. I wrote to the Taoiseach myself, enclosing my appointee's cv and informed him of the appointment. There were some unhappy bunnies in the Department when they discovered this. The reason for the stalling was, without any doubt, the fact that the appointment of new junior ministers was in the offing and that they hoped I would not be among those re-appointed to the Department by Brian Cowen. Indeed, they may have already picked up on their Minister's position on that.

It was a small but satisfying goodbye present.

I had been in the Department almost two years. I had enjoyed a great deal of my work and given the position my best shot, obviously good enough to get me sacked. On the way out I waved at Brendan the Navigator on the wall of the Department, but he didn't notice, he was too busy pulling red tape off his compass.

Chapter 10 ~

GLOBAL HORSE-TRADING

As I pointed out earlier, the position of Minister of State for Trade and Commerce came with some specific roles and responsibilities. Perhaps the most important of these are representing and selling Ireland abroad, promoting exports and meetings with trade ministers from the EU and elsewhere. Along with Enterprise Ireland, the Department supports exports through international trade shows and exhibitions. I was responsible for negotiating Ireland's case in the marathon ongoing deliberation on the Doha round of the World Trade Organization (WTO) talks that, although interesting, were very demanding, particularly because I wanted to fully understand Ireland's position.

My first trade mission with Enterprise Ireland was to Dubai for a technology trade fair on 31 August 2007. I was there to represent and support seven Enterprise Ireland clients who were actively pursuing business in the Middle East. It was a long trip—16 hours—and I had to prepare speeches, receive briefings and attend meetings with Enterprise Ireland officials and representatives of the companies, as well as being present at the trade fair. I was accompanied by a number of officials from the Department, my private secretary Eamonn McCormack, and Enterprise Ireland representatives.

What normally happens is that Enterprise Ireland arranges whatever is going on, usually with help from the relevant embassy, and then the Minister backs them up by attending and speaking at functions and meetings, encouraging and supporting the exporters and interacting with their clients.

I think the number of officials accompanying a Minister on most trips should be no more than two, including a Minister's private secretary. One informed official, along with Enterprise Ireland or IDA personnel, with local embassy staff providing backup, is enough for all but the most extraordinary meetings. I was regularly accompanied by many more and I don't know how many travel with Cabinet ministers, but all have to be fed and watered using taxpayers' money.

It's not easy work, because time is usually short, jetlag is often involved and a speech must be prepared. I usually write my own, which again troubled the Department that, at the beginning, provided me with scripts packed with statistics and numbers— Valium bricks, the likes of which bore businessmen at conferences around the world. Individuals and companies serious about doing business with us already know all that, or will easily get it from the Department, local embassies or Enterprise Ireland.

I'd take out what little I needed from the Department's effort for my speech, try to establish a relaxed connection with my audience and, essentially, tell them that we want their business and that Enterprise Ireland, myself and the Department would help in any way we could. And I tried to use a few words of the local language. Afterwards, I worked the room, speaking to people on a one-to-one basis to drive the message home.

It worked well and I think officials began to realise that my speeches did not give away any trade or State secrets, like our nuclear capability or the recipe for Irish Mist, although they were never happy about not having control.

These trips often brought me into contact with our ambassadors and their staff. I admire the work they do and I don't think I've ever been at an embassy function where I wasn't proud to be Irish, even if once or twice an ambassador and I had a polite discussion about where diplomacy ended and government began.

Critical media reports about ministers travelling abroad are often wide of the mark. Although talk about the Government jet and grand hotels conjures up visions of the high life, in reality it's generally far from that. Doing the job properly involves a lot of preparation, the journeys are often long and, while I might miss Michael O'Leary being there to weigh my bag and welcome me aboard, a Government jet is a plane, and a hotel room is a place to sleep off jetlag. And then there is always the absence of family. I enjoyed the challenges of the work and the rare moments when I could take time to look at where I was. But usually it's about meetings, functions, a meal with Eamonn or officials and a long flight back.

I watched the John O'Donoghue saga with interest and I felt that the fact that ministers' trips abroad are usually arranged by officials, with ministers generally uninvolved, did not get an airing. Certainly, no official stood up to explain the whys and wherefores of the arrangements that had been made. I am not saying that John O'Donoghue did not have questions to answer, but the fact is that the officials travelling with him would have had more or less the same arrangements that they were organising for the Minister. The lack of tension between officials and politicians to which I keep referring can work both ways. The Minister should have noticed the extravagance, but the officials making bookings for him should have been aware of the expense, the breach of guidelines and the political dangers.

I used the Government jet a number of times to and from Baldonnell. I didn't involve myself in the arranging of trips in any way, assuming that the officials who did that work would do it properly and cost-effectively. I stayed in good hotels, which was necessary for Ireland's image, rather than my desire for luxury. I didn't notice anything that might have encouraged me to question cost. I just presumed that standard controls and procedures were in place.

In December 2007, I felt confident enough of my knowledge to make a presentation on the stalled WTO talks, which were expected to resume in 2008, to the Oireachtas Committee on Enterprise and Small Business. I was convinced that farming, and beef in particular, would be central to those talks and our negotiating position. My increasing knowledge of the complex issues involved was as a result of meetings I was having with some excellent civil servants, Gerry Monks and Sabha Greene.

Gerry Monks knew everything about the operation of the WTO and knew the intricacies of the talks process. His colleague, Sabha Greene, sketched out for me, in different coloured markers, the layered structures of the WTO, noting the various pillars that made up the negotiations, the different live issues and the positions of each party at the talks. She was a mine of information and had an exceptional knowledge of the minutiae.

It was a complex matter to understand but you cannot do a good job if you don't know what you are doing. I felt it was essential that I had a comprehensive grasp of the situation because at negotiations you need to be able to think fast on your feet and know what questions to ask. Gerry and Sabha had me well prepared in a short space of time.

Our meetings in Europe were about what Peter Mandelson would do when he went as the EU's representative to the Doha round of the WTO talks. Every country in Europe wanted its position defended. Ireland was a small player so, broadly speaking, we had to forge allegiances with bigger European countries that either had interests aligned with ours, like France, with its strong and vocal agricultural sector, or with which we could trade support positions. Take away the complex rules and regulations and you discover a horse-trading fair at which the boys from Ballinasloe would not be lost. I wasn't going to be either.

Gerry advised that it was critical I should travel to meet my counterparts, particularly in Europe, since there had been no Council of Ministers meetings since my appointment. This was important, not just to introduce me, but to make a strong statement about Ireland's negotiating position.

Gerry and Eamonn planned a programme that took us to various European capitals, starting in London and moving on to Geneva, Brussels, Lublijana, The Hague and Paris. There were also meetings with trade ministers as well as Peter Mandelson, the EU Trade Commissioner, and Paschal Lamy, the Director General of the WTO, and the itinerary was agreed for early 2008.

I had no great concern about meeting these heavy hitters. I was well prepared, knew my brief and the people involved were politicians, whose attitudes and agendas are the same all over the world. The meetings were going to be about finding common ground, building relationships and achieving results that worked for both parties—polite horse-trading.

I was also armed with information I had acquired from sources other than officials. I had made contact with the Irish Farmers' Association (IFA), which had their own highly efficient network in Brussels and a position that differed from the Department's and our officials in Brussels.

My first meeting was with Gareth Thomas, the British Parliamentary Undersecretary of Trade and Consumer Affairs. It was interesting. I suppose it is informative and sometimes exciting for officials to accompany ministers to meetings, a necessary break from the day-to-day business of law-making, rule designing and the scratch of quill on vellum. But if Moses could carry tablets of stone down the mountain alone, surely to God only a Minister on a life-saving machine needs 6 or 10 assistants to pull a few political rabbits out of a hat.

I always travelled with Eamonn, a mine of information and a great support. To cover the unlikely event that politicians I was meeting strayed into some impenetrable thicket of Eurospeak with which I was not familiar, I needed and was happy to have either or both Gerry Monks and Sabha Greene with me, and a representative from the local embassy ready to pour unctions from the diplomatic bag on any wounds I might inflict on the largely impervious hides of the politicians I was jousting with. Four expert first aid personnel is quite enough.

On the day I met Gareth Thomas, there were eight of them, all armed with Blackberrys, on which, I later learned, they spent much time discussing my body language and that of my opposite number (do we not have a law against this?) and quite useless commentary about nuances. I went into that meeting with the four encyclopedias I needed and four book ends. At the other side there was Thomas and, I think, three officials. This was a regular feature of meetings I attended in Europe and it was entirely unnecessary and, in a way, damaging.

It might have been amusing if the Irish people weren't paying for it and the strength of my personal position was not being undermined by the appearance that I needed half the Irish Civil Service to support me.

The look of incredulity on the faces of Gareth Thomas and his officials as my bush of Blackberrys came through the door was bad enough, but then I had to suffer during the first few minutes of our meeting while my host tried to politely establish if I was brain-dead or a certifiable lunatic under close supervision. Once Thomas had decided that I was no risk to him or his officials, in a move that caught me by surprise but was very welcome, he turned to my Blackberry bush and asked the eight of them to leave as well as his three, underlining my point about the necessity of it all.

That said, the meetings went well. The British weren't much interested in agriculture, a sector that is an increasingly small part of their economy. But there was goodwill.

From London, we travelled on to Geneva to meet Paschal Lamy, Director General of the wto; Ambassador De Amateo of Mexico; Don Stevenson from Canada, who was the chairman of the negotiating group on non-agricultural market access; and Crawford Falconer from New Zealand, who was chairman of the agriculture negotiating group. We then travelled to Berlin, Slovenia, The Hague and Paris in just a few hectic days to meet the trade ministers together with Irish diplomats from our embassies.

It became clear to me as I travelled through Europe that there was a disconnect between Ireland's official and political positions on what we wanted out of the WTO talks. It seemed to me, and I think the IFA and the Irish Exporters Association shared my view, that officials were not willing to aggressively defend Irish agriculture and were not clear either about our general economic interests, described as the services pillar of the talks.

The IFA has a reputation for being one of the most effective lobby groups in Brussels. Its permanent representative there is Michael Treacy, a man who is highly regarded for his deep and intimate knowledge of the European Union's agriculture operation and the fine detail of the WTO negotiations. I had developed a good relationship with the IFA locally in Carlow-Kilkenny as well as nationally with its president, Padraig Walsh and the president elect John Bryan. It was essential that I meet Michael.

The Doha round was in its sixth year and it was becoming clear that it would have to be brought to a close soon if we wanted to effect the main purpose of the round, which was to offer assistance to less developed countries. Behind the scenes, the IFA and other farming organisations were ratcheting up their campaign to have their case heard. John Bryan had led a delegation of beef farmers to South America to investigate the beef industry there. Their concern was that Ireland's hugely important beef industry would be under threat from imports of cheap beef from South America that did not have to comply with the same stringent standards applied to European beef.

No Minister can afford not to have an informed and reasonable understanding of his brief. While officials might like the control it gives them, it doesn't help them or the country in the long run, because they have to step into a risk-taking and decision-making role that they are not trained for and, by their nature, they are generally not comfortable with. Much of what happened to Ireland over the past four or five years, in my opinion, was caused by these management flaws and malfunctions. It was the Peter

Principle in operation: people being promoted to, or having to fill, positions beyond their experience, competence or inclination.

Furthermore, officials abroad can end up as supporters of or hostages to the prevailing bureaucratic culture. In Brussels, for example, they can become 'good Europeans'. It is for this reason that some British politicians call the Foreign Office, the 'foreigners' office'. As our history books tell us in relation to the Normans: 'more Irish than the Irish themselves'.

The phenomenon I describe as drift applies equally to uninformed ministers involved in long negotiations. Over time, they allow themselves to be persuaded by the official line, the line of least resistance for them. They can be too influenced by the belief that Ireland is, after all, just a small nation on the periphery of Europe, which can weaken resolve in negotiations regarding the WTO talks and other agreements.

I am unsure about how deep and extensive the briefings given to senior ministers are. I can only say that I came into my Department without a briefing and I had considerable responsibilities. When I left with, admittedly, an unusual amount of information because of my interest, I was not debriefed by the Department or the incoming Minister and there was no handover period. That is lunacy and an indication of the Department's view of the contribution a Minister makes.

Ministers should be met, introduced to senior civil servants and briefed, if necessary for days, involving a handover by the outgoing Minister on their responsibilities, with any major known problem being brought to their attention. Their office and general staff should be in place or, at least, candidates ready for interview. There should be no delay in getting the Minister up and running. The current absence of these protocols demonstrates better than any words of mine what senior civil servants think of their political masters. It also reflects badly on what those politicians think of themselves. Or was it just me who experienced all this neglect?

No Minister can afford to just listen to the official position and it is often better not to have officials at meetings at which you are doing this, apart, sometimes, from your personal private secretary, who might take minutes. There are at least two good reasons for this. First, the individual organisation you are talking to is usually a client of the Department and may well be unwilling to open up in front of officials, indeed, may fear reprisals. The second reason is you do not want officials guiding conversations and taking some official action regarding them later.

Officials do not like being left out of the loop, because it means loss of control, although they claim that it is for the Minister's own good. Balderdash. It is for the good of the Department. Certainly, my regular meetings throughout my term to hear opinions and take soundings annoyed them. But I was a Minister and if I took a decision, on best official advice, and it went badly wrong, no official would be collecting his or her P45 along with me. The fact that I got my P45 largely for behaving as a Minister should, makes the point. And we all know now just how sound 'best advice' is.

In EU politics and diplomacy, the officials are often called 'sherpas' after the Tibetan mountain men who do all the hard work scaling Mount Everest, so that the highly equipped mountaineers who come after them can breeze up the slope with ease. These elite civil servants, who regard themselves as the crème-de-la-crème of their departments, prepare all the official positions and documentation and expect the ministers to breeze in at the last minute and sign everything off. I don't do breeze-ins and I don't sign off on what I don't understand. It might leave me freezing on top of a mountain, which is why mountaineers always check their own ropes.

My meeting with Michael Treacy of the IFA was an enlightening one. He had complete control of his brief and was fully supportive of the position I was about to take on behalf of Ireland. To a large extent my view reflected the IFA position, even though there were some areas of disagreement. The civil servants from the Department were disappointed I cut loose to have the meeting with Treacy, but I felt it was essential to have his unmediated view on exactly where we stood. In addition to Gerry Monks and Sabha Greene, I would rely heavily on Michael Treacy for information on how to approach the WTO talks for the optimum benefit for Ireland.

I shared with the IFA a determination that the beef industry in Ireland would not go the same route as the sugar beet industry—a sector that had been very important to Irish agriculture and to the communities, including Carlow, in which the sugar factories were located. I believe that we should have been able to retain it—we just didn't stand up for it strongly enough. I believe the officials dealing with the negotiations in Brussels allowed themselves to drift into underestimating the impact on Ireland of the loss of sugar beet. In a human sense, civil servants living in Brussels need to be seen by their international colleagues as 'good Europeans'. They may have been so much part of the system and thinking in Europe that they underestimated the consequences of their actions at home.

The EU is undoubtedly a great idea but politically and, therefore, economically it is a family of very different personalities. The hot south and the cold north—rationality and passion—don't sit easily together, as recent events have shown in the arguments about budgetary control. No official or Minister should be seduced by the idea so much as to forget Ireland's interest and we should remember that Britain's long view has kept it out of the currency, not that I am suggesting it isn't a good idea for Ireland. To paraphrase Cromwell: 'Trust in the EU, but keep your country safe.'

That, incidentally, is not an anti-European position. It's just common sense.

Over a period of time, I prepared with Eamonn, Gerry and Sabha for what was to prove a pivotal meeting with Peter Mandelson in Brussels on 21 February. Its purpose was to present the Irish Government's definitive position on the trade talks, particularly in terms of what we were and weren't prepared to concede on agriculture and services. The atmosphere was charged because Irish famers had a perception that Peter Mandelson was about to sell them out—agriculture in Britain is no longer that important to its economy. As part of the process, I issued press statements indicating that I intended to harden my stance on behalf of Irish farmers. Mandelson also had quite a reputation and there was a certain fascination—Prince of Darkness, Lord of Spin, etc. etc. I was looking forward to meeting him as, no doubt, was my Blackberry bush.

When we arrived at Mandelson's office in the Berlaymont Building for the meeting, he was somewhat taken aback at the posse accompanying me—there were 12 in total. 'Thank you for meeting us, Commissioner Mandelson,' I said. 'I bring greetings from the IFA.' He laughed and the ice was broken. However, throughout the meeting he was bemused at the Blackberry bush behind me, on which not a leaf whispered throughout our exchanges. He was charming to deal with. Clearly, he had been given my cv as he mentioned that we had both been first elected to local authorities in 1979: him to Lambeth Borough Council and me to Kilkenny Corporation. Our progress thereafter was somewhat different!

The meeting lasted about 45 minutes and we discussed all the issues around Ireland's role in the WTO talks. I made a strong case for Ireland and emphasised that we had taken a position in relation to agriculture and would not be deviating from it.

There was an assumption among the officials in Brussels that what we might lose on agriculture in the WTO talks would be made up for with concessions on the services pillar, which covers sectors like IT, insurance, banking, etc. However, I was convinced, from speaking to the IFA, that we needed to hold on to everything in the agriculture pillar because it is so vital to our economy. There was little sense in doing otherwise as, if nothing else, it was a bargaining chip. Furthermore, the services pillar was not looking promising—it was not developed and did not have any real content so the danger was we could be about to buy a pig in a poke. On behalf of Ireland, I had no intention of allowing Mandelson to proceed in the WTO negotiations as he intended. It simply would not be in the country's interests.

We were not in a strong position, so we were relying on our traditional friendship with France and Germany to support Ireland as a small nation. Behind the scenes, we met the other delegations to see where they were and develop new friendships and support.

Prior to a General Affairs meeting on 18 July, I met at the offices of the Irish Permanent Representation with Ambassador Bobby McDonagh to discuss the approach to that meeting. He had a script in his hand and the officials, I think, had been pressing their case with him. With the effortless superiority that Balliol men are famous for, he confronted me when I told him his script did not fit with my previously stated position, which I believed was in Ireland's best interest, nor did it contain any comment on what Peter Mandelson and Angela Merkel had said about the Irish position. I told him I was rejecting it. During the course of preparing another script, Kilkenny CBS and Oxford had a heated discussion. I would not draw back from my position that we needed a much stronger message. Dick Roche, the Minister of State with responsibility for European Affairs, in fact, pointed out to Bobby that I was the Minister and, therefore, the decision was mine—the CBS had been joined by UCD! I got a script of sorts, but as I was delivering it I could say what I liked. And I did.

At the General Affairs meeting, I said what I wanted to say and believed I was right. Afterwards there was a press briefing at which the officials decided to stand at the back of the room. They were not going to join me at the table and take questions, obviously angry at the position that I had taken. I was joined by Dick Roche, in a gesture of support that I appreciated, but I had the knowledge to handle the questions without any problem.

I also did an interview in the corridor with RTÉ News during which I reiterated my intention to aggressively defend the position of Ireland, with a view to getting a balanced deal, not sacrificing any more on beef or farming and demanding that the other pillars, such as services, which were critical to Ireland, should be developed in a more rounded way.

It was quite interesting recently to hear Brian Cowen talk about the importance of agriculture to Ireland and the billions that could be generated from it, a position I have long held. It vindicates my actions in Brussels and demonstrates again the need for ministers to take leadership roles by questioning and checking the opinions, beliefs and policies of their departments.

In July, a ministerial meeting in Geneva was scheduled and then cancelled as no agreement was seen as possible. Finally, a ministerial meeting was called on 22 July and this time it seemed there was a clear intention on the part of Mandelson and Lamy to bring the talks to a successful conclusion.

After being in Geneva for a while, the IFA and the Irish Exporters Association thought a deal was imminent. I thought otherwise— there were too many unresolved issues: Germany worried about its car industry; Ireland, France, Spain and Italy about the protection of their respective agriculture sectors, particularly regarding the flooding of European markets with South American beef. Meanwhile, other countries had issues around bananas!

Remarkably, very little was said about the emerging less developed countries and the need to protect them in global trade, given that this was the purpose of the WTO Doha round. Instead, the focus was on the individual requirements of European countries and other WTO countries. They all demanded concessions as the talks progressed, the main feature of which was outright protectionism. The whole process was dressed up to look sophisticated and complicated. It involved ministers, ambassadors and heads of state but ultimately it amounted to nothing more than buying a horse at a fair: a deal and a handshake.

Mandelson's position had been progressively weakened as he had to accede to more and more concessions to individual European member states. Every time he returned to the French-chaired meetings he had to recalibrate his negotiating position on behalf of the European Union. I wondered why the conscientious and conservative Paschal Lamy should have called the talks in the first place.

We held our position, continued side meetings with the IFA and tried to steer and influence Mary Coughlan, who had just been transferred from the Department of Agriculture to Enterprise, Trade and Employment, and the current Agriculture Minister, Brendan Smith, neither of whom, in fairness, had had time to be fully briefed and, again, were in the hands of their officials.

It is essential to have a strong team of senior public servants and politicians at the talks, but there was too much duplication and too much of them reinforcing one another's views. The exclusion of the IFA, the Irish Exporters Association and other stakeholders was a bad move. A small crack team, including those representative bodies, with —I believed—their better intelligence would have worked much more efficiently and effectively. There was, as a result, a tension between me and senior ministers, which wasn't helpful. I did an interview with CNN, which had been set up by officials in Dublin, outlining the state of play, which seemed to upset everyone around me, yet all I did was express my known position.

The IFA was on the periphery in Geneva, excluded, I feel, because senior civil servants want control and will not engage at a meaningful level with anyone who challenges their fixed ideas. This isn't what should happen.

The Irish delegation comprised the Tánaiste, Mary Coughlan; the Minister for Agriculture, Brendan Smith; Peter Power, the Minister of State for Overseas Development; and myself as Minister of State for Trade and Commerce. Of those, I was the only politician among the Irish delegation to take an independent line with officials, largely because of the knowledge and experience I had acquired during my time dealing with the wto. Geneva was swamped by Irish officials.

We spent 10 days in Geneva talking and negotiating. It was like scout camp, with code words for the conversations like 'the green room', 'walks in the woods', and so on. Most of the serious debate, discussion and agreements happened outside the main room, which was the theatre of the process. Peter Mandelson was continually asked to come back from the wto talks to explain what he had done, what he was about to do and if he had given anything away. I know that he was particularly uncomfortable with that but it was the only way we could ensure that he would not surrender the interests of the European Union and, in particular, the smaller countries.

The anticipation was that because it was a development round, the agreement would be ready for signature in December in Doha, but that never materialised, as I anticipated. Ultimately, no agreement was reached, to the consternation and annoyance of many officials, and we all went home.

I felt that my stance had been vindicated and that we upheld and strengthened our position, so that if and when there is a renewed attempt to reach agreement on the wto Doha round, Ireland's interests will have been well served by our work. The ifa and *Farmers' Journal* reports were favourable. At the heart of this was a clash of style. Some senior ministers were prepared to drift with officials and work gently on positions whereas I was determined to lead rather than be led.

In general, the talks made for great theatre but our part in them did not impress me. Any future talks should be based on a more focused strategy. We should limit numbers and organise the delegation in tiers. Ireland plc should have an established formal forum for all the interested parties to come together and nominate a small crack team of negotiators, with the Minister and a senior official at its head.

At a time of world economic crisis, there is a need for a dynamic global trade agreement that can contribute to the stability of banks, banking regulation, businesses and transfer of people across the world. Crises in the agricultural, banking and automotive sectors, for example, could all be helped by a more flexible working relationship in terms of tariffs throughout the world, making trade easier. A world trade agreement should be a target of any Government in terms of international relations. Ireland should be the leading country within the EU to demand a conclusion to the Doha round.

The problem is that the Doha round was already dated by the time we were discussing it in Geneva. It had already been six years in the making and the conclusions that were being sought were solutions to old problems. In the meantime, new problems were emerging. We must now rapidly and dynamically tackle those issues and put in a modern framework to deal with modern trade and its major social impacts. Ireland should demand this action because it includes assistance to countries that need it so much. We must fulfil a socio-economic obligation and create a lasting framework and a solution to the WTO talks and an agreement.

There was an attempt to isolate me in the course of those talks but, because of my understanding and knowledge of the subject, my input could not be excluded. I also knew that it was a source of annoyance to everyone that I had made the effort to meet all of the others who were outside the loop in order to show that somebody did understand and was taking their views into account.

If the game was to be played out again, I would still hold the strong position that I held then and I would include all of those people, all of those stakeholders, in the talks, because the best information I got came from the exporters' group, the IFA and the other farming lobbies.

Horse-trading needs traders, people who can tangle, confuse, argue and think fast, spit on their hands and do the deal. Next time we should send some of the boys from Ballinasloe.

Chapter 11 ∿

| FOXES AND HENS

Just two weeks before the banking system was brought to its knees, precipitating the worst financial crisis this country has ever experienced, I was invited to address the Beverage Council of Ireland's annual conference on 12 September 2008. Mary Coughlan couldn't attend the event so I agreed to accept the invitation in her absence. As it was a gathering of business people largely representing the SME sector, I decided to use the event to lay out my stall and outline my experiences in the Department.

The general knowledge from my political life, my membership of Dáil committees, vice-chairmanship of the Public Accounts Committee and my experiences in the Department were drawn upon. I set down my position, where I felt politicians and officials were failing, the role of unions and the need for change. I expected the speech to provoke debate and political and union reaction and I hoped that it would bring about much-needed change.

I was not prepared for what was to follow.

For the record, this is the full text of the speech I delivered that morning. Before I began, I did explain to the gathering that, while I was there instead of Mary Coughlan, the speech I was about to give was not hers and the views being expressed were my own and, therefore, carried a health warning. It will come as no surprise that, unlike the many speeches delivered by ministers over the years, this one is absent from the archive on the website of the Department of Enterprise, Trade and Innovation, perhaps because they did not write it! I will supply them with a copy so that their records are complete.

After centuries of depression, the Irish entered the promised land. Not only was there milk and honey, there were bankers who were prepared to lend and lend to builders who wanted to build and build and sell to a public who wanted to buy and buy. Not just in Bundoran and west Cork, but Bulgaria and west Africa. On top of that, politicians and public servants found themselves handling billions with the same abacus, mind set and systems that they had used for generations to count ha'pennies during times when an Irish traffic jam consisted of men on bikes on the way to the labour exchange.

Those men and their wives, sons and daughters needed a party and probably deserved one. Indeed a party was unavoidable given the level of euphoria and optimism in the country, which was even greater than the depression we are all feeling now that the party is over. So where is post-party Ireland? When the hangover clears, we will still be far better off than before. We will also be wiser and more careful and we will learn from our mistakes. But some of the liaisons and arrangements made during party time will have to be substantially altered or discarded.

Mistakes are signposts telling us which direction to travel in future, if we are to be safe. We could do well to consider them and heed the message. We should understand that much of what is now happening was unavoidable. We just added our desire to party and our lust for property to the flames. Tectonic shifts are taking place in the world: economically, socially and climatically. We have the influence of the huge BRIC economies of Brazil, Russia, India and China consuming basic resources or controlling them with an endless supply of cheap labour on call. Massive demand and aspiration will make these countries, indeed is making these countries, potent forces in the world.

Basic resources and food prices will never again be as cheap as they were.

Add to this the credit crunch, global warming, the silent battles for water, the continuing slow decline of western manufacturing and the growing power of technology, which is turning the world into a single inter-related marketplace and you have a powerful unstable cocktail, which will take time to settle and which heralds the beginning of a new, very different world. Any two of these events would normally be enough to cause upheaval. Altogether they caused mayhem and reminded us forcefully just how small and vulnerable we are in Ireland.

What can we do about it? Let's start with last Sunday's All Ireland hurling final and the two before that. I probably wouldn't use this comparison if Kilkenny had lost, in fact I might not even have come here! We take losing hard in Kilkenny—and that's the point.

Kilkenny has won three All Irelands because everyone on the field is a master and gives 100%. If they don't, or if they are not good enough, or if they can't take the heat, they are taken off or dropped. Brian Cody picks the man most qualified for each position and expects performance. He is the boss, he has won All-Ireland medals himself so he knows what he is doing and his small number of advisers and selectors are also pro-fessional, diligent and demanding.

That is how you win All Irelands, contracts, promotion or markets. You pursue excellence relentlessly, you innovate; you pick the best; you keep it lean and mean; you reward success and starve failure or mediocrity, and you treat everyone equally. Facing into its own battles, how does Ireland measure up to these standards? What advantages do we have? What should we concentrate on? What have we to do to be better?

Ireland has three great advantages. It has a working population of two million, 20% of whom are employed by the State. Our people are relatively well-educated. We are no larger

than a large multinational. We should be able to turn on a six-
pence, to retool and retrain. We should be able to trim our sails
quickly when prevailing conditions demand it. Our second
advantage is the extraordinary network of Irish people and
people of Irish descent around the world: children of the
diaspora, some of them in very senior positions, who promote
in various ways a positive image of this country. They give us
an edge that many countries envy.

I have often felt that this resource has not been sufficiently
recognised or nurtured. I believe that each country should over
time build a database of its connections throughout the world
that it can look to for information, support and help. Finally,
we are an energetic, adventurous and creative race. We have
punched above our weight in the marketplaces of the world for
many years. Our businessmen have enormous experience and
have proven themselves against the best.

But to continue the sporting metaphor, the problem for
Ireland is that while our midfield and forwards are giving 100%
and scoring goals, our backs are just not up to the task. They
are not supplying good ball and they are leaking scores, some
of them own goals. Worse still, they cannot be taken off. Brian
Cody would have a heart attack.

I have been told many times that I am outspoken, as if there
is something wrong with being frank. Certainly in politics it is
sometimes wiser to tread softly, but not all the time and not
when the leadership role that all politicians have accepted
demands straight talking. Too much can be lost in translation
in a thicket of euphemisms and blandness. I will speak frankly
now.

The public service is the back office of this country. It spends
money hard-earned by others. At its higher levels it should be
advising ministers, bringing forward initiatives and indeed
restraining short term political impulses. It is honest, impartial
and full of good people. But it is now so over-protected by its

unions that it has largely become a reactionary, inert mass at the centre of our economy. Its culture destroys ambition, resists change and is now so insulated from reality that inform- ation can be withheld from a Minister, unfavourable reports are doctored and answers to parliamentary questions that come too close to the bone are masterclasses in obfuscation which can deny our TDS the information they need to get to the heart of the matter.

This culture protects the sacred inner sanctum where the status quo is venerated and the mantra 'men may come and men may go, but we go on forever!' is frequently heard. One of the results of all this is that many professional positions in the public service, like those in HR or internal auditing, are not filled by professionally qualified people, because promotion is all too often based on longevity rather than by ability or qualification, if indeed people with the necessary qualifications can be found. As a consequence, there are far too many well- paid but unhappy square pegs in round holes throughout the public service. Furthermore, most state institutions are not subject to many of the controls and regulations which are hung around the necks of private individuals and commercial enterprises.

All State and semi-State bodies should be ISO compliant. Professional positions should be filled by professionals. All departments should be audited annually by external auditing firms reporting to the Comptroller and Auditor General's office. All procurement of stationery, equipment, advertising and so on should be done through one office, again under the control of the Comptroller and Auditor General.

I am particularly concerned by the fact that the public service continues to employ, adding more and more people who are almost impossible to let go and who will in due course be getting inflation-proof salaries and pensions. In today's world this is madness if it was ever sensible and I believe the

Government should tell the unions that the pay and conditions of new employees will be substantially different, thereby drawing a line under an arrangement that I consider an abuse of the taxes paid by the owners and workers in the private sector.

The State and its employees should broadly be subject to the same rules and regulations as everyone else. If this is not done, we are running a two-tier Ireland. We are reinforcing the belief that there is something exceptional, something a cut above the rest about being an employee of the State. That attitude, the lack of accountability, the lack of professionalism and the virtual impossibility of being sacked is destructive. It steals individuality, encourages arrogance, forces compliance to a culture, drains enthusiasm and denies the people, the politicians and the wealth creators of this country the benefits of a modern, high powered creative arm of the State that is vital to our continued success. The public service has to be immediately, radically overhauled because we cannot afford it in its present form. Do we need to discuss FÁS? Are there others that we will audit after millions more have bolted?

All of this, according to the press, has encouraged a group of civic minded senior civil servants to take the unprecedented step of demanding change. They are right. They should keep it up. They are doing all of us a service and we should stand up with them and for them and so should any of their colleagues who share their views.

I certainly will continue to stand up because it is my duty. Plain language is needed and change is urgently required. If we continue to permit our public service to act in a Corinthian manner—in both meanings of the word—we are binding the arms and damaging the morale of those who are driving this country forward. And I am not talking here about the people at the coalface: the nurses, doctors, gardaí, teachers, and others who keep a failing system going against the odds.

For five years I sat on the Public Accounts Committee with my businessman's hat on watching, with certain exceptions like the Revenue Commissioners, a procession of representatives of boards and bodies peering into a series of black holes, completely unable to explain the mystery of it all, but content that no one would lose his job over it.

Featherless but still plump State hens, puzzled by what had happened when they tangled with swift, suave commercial foxes. People who have never feared for their jobs, fought with their bank managers, worried about their businesses, confronted competition or battled with red tape simply do not understand. Well-meaning, bright but inexperienced, they are unlikely to play a blinder for Ireland or understand how to help those who do. Meanwhile, the private sector complains of red tape, delay, unwieldy laws, lack of understanding and complacency from individuals and organisations whose job should surely be to support, encourage and assist, at speed.

But maybe something has happened. Ireland has created a new dance. You don't need to be nimble on your feet. In fact activity is not encouraged, nor do you need to be creative, passionate or exciting. It's the very opposite of the tango. It's the quango. And you get paid for doing it, by the public who are now becoming doubtful about the purpose of it all. We have far too many quangos putting bums on seats instead of putting ideas on the table. A significant number of them form the hidden scaffolding around the social partnership and that scaffolding should be torn down because largely it is not now working, at least for the country.

Yes, I know government over time established many of these organisations. We thought it was a good idea. It separated politicians from some things they could be blamed for interfering with. It wasn't a good idea. Our job is to interfere, question, control, take responsibility and give leadership, admit to mistakes and do U-turns when necessary. We should do a U-turn now. We should close and downsize quangos as necessary and appoint professionals on to the reduced boards of those we keep and demand results and accountability.

We need Brian Cody to roar 'get off the field all those holding the hurley at the wrong end'. So, having identified some problems, what should we be doing to keep Ireland moving? Everything starts with education and in today's world you ain't going to the top without it. And even then, to really succeed you need qualifications that are internationally recognised hallmarks of excellence. You also need languages and we need to do something about the fact that we are way behind other countries in the number that we speak.

Stand up anyone over 50 who believes the exams their children are passing and the degrees they are obtaining are anything like as hard as they were in your time. You can take equality too far. Everyone in Kilkenny doesn't get to play on the team. Excellence and exceptionality is recognised and encouraged. If we want to go on succeeding on the world stage, our schools, from primary up to university, will have to find ways of developing and challenging our Ph.D prospects and maybe that means that the educational bar has to be raised everywhere, which would be no bad thing. It is now at too low a level generally.

We should immediately begin the process of preparing for nuclear energy because that is what we'll be using whether we like it or not, wind, wave and solar energy notwithstanding. We should immediately do everything possible to make the IFSC more attractive to foreign companies and prepare ourselves for more tax competition from other countries. Services like those provided in the IFSC are essential to our success. We should look at and fully understand how valuable the green image of Ireland is and strengthen our tourism initiatives, particularly in rural pursuits like hunting, riding and fishing. We need to continue to help our farmers to add value to their produce and here again the green image of Ireland is something they should concentrate on.

I have no fear about immigration, but immigrants coming to this country should clearly know that they enter, legitimately seeking self-improvement, on our terms. Ireland is a country that has its roots firmly in European culture and tradition. We guarantee religious freedom, but we do not intend to change our values, regulations or culture, or permit outside the home the promotion of or insistence on standards or positions that will impede reasonable integration of other nationalities into our society.

Our enterprise boards must find new and better ways of encouraging and training potential entrepreneurs and businesspeople, involving business leaders and companies where possible. Nothing succeeds like success and providing role models is a first step in that direction. Kilkenny has won three All-Irelands and this year may win a fourth. Last Sunday evening, kids were emulating their heroes on pitches throughout the county, taking the first steps on the path of achievement, fair competition and excellence.

I am tired of committees with big names and small achievements. I'm a businessman so I know about keeping it simple, professional and tight. I don't want to listen to or read ambiguous expensive consultants' reports. The wastepaper baskets of the world are full of them. I don't mind hearing or considering the unpalatable. I don't mind taking risks. I don't believe in rules that frustrate the 95% who are compliant for the 5% who are not. I am not a fan of big government. I am not in this job to get on. I am in this job because I want to make a difference. That means I have to speak out when I see the need for change.

Members of the Dáil are the board of Ireland Limited and the Government heads that board. Ours is the responsibility and we should not shy from it. Over the last number of years far too much power has been handed to virtually unaccountable bodies of one sort or another. Elites have grown up some of which believe themselves to be beyond political influence—think what that means—and maybe even above political control.

In a rush of guilt to the head because of a few bad apples we gave away too much. We should now take it back. Ireland is not a bureaucracy. It should be run by the representatives of the people and they too should be sacked if they are not good enough. Societies are founded on enlightened self-interest. We limit our freedom as individuals to gain the strength and protection of the group and then live under the banners of republicanism, liberalism, communism or whatever. Ireland is a republic: power is vested in the people and their elected representatives. All are equal before the law and maybe that's where equality stops.

There can be no equality in a country where a significant number of those who spend public money enjoy wages and conditions far more favourable than those who create the wealth of this country, protected by unions whose own self-interest is best served by keeping their members in golden cages, refusing to pull aside the blanket of protectionism so that they can participate in a world which may be more challenging but will also be more exciting, enriching and surprisingly gratifying than the protected, unrealistic space they currently occupy at considerable cost to themselves and the nation.

We will know that change has taken place, real genuine change when there is a healthy two-way flow between all levels of public service and private sector employment. That is the only benchmark worth having. What we need to do is concentrate on Best Practice Ireland, in politics, in public service, in business and in society. I believe in progress and the right of people to make the best they can of themselves. But I also believe that progress needs to be careful where it puts its feet.

There are people out there, our people who do not march to the sound of urgent frantic drummers. They are the mild, the old, the sick and those who cannot or, let us be honest, do not want to work. No civilized society should ignore or reject these people. They should not be on trolleys in corridors or given public money without care and respect while at the same time, millions and millions of public money disappears down black holes and no one goes down the black hole after it. We are in danger in this country of leaving too many behind in our headlong march towards material success and that must not happen.

Let's get Best Practice Ireland going. I don't like Michael O'Leary going on a rant but he has made a world-class airline. He should be asked to join the board of Best Practice Ireland along with others like Peter Sutherland, Dermot Desmond, Gerry Robinson and Denis O'Brien who have demonstrated to the world what Irish people can do when we put our minds to it. I am willing to bet that they will produce recommendations within a month on less than ten pages. I am not willing to bet that we will be allowed to act on them. 'Yes, Minister' lives on.

The unions too must play their part, not in capitulation but in cooperation and contribution, redefining the job they do for their members and understanding the job they can do for their country. Best Practice Ireland must start with patriotism; the greatest and most honourable of the children of enlightened self-interest. What we need to do now, perhaps more than anything, is the understanding that we are all in this together. Together we need to urgently respond to great global challenges, and that will require new initiatives from everybody.

If Ireland is to keep its place and grow in the global marketplace we will have to be patriotic and if there isn't a template we should make our own. We have come far but our success has overtaken some of our institutions. They need to renew themselves and take their place on a team that can take on the world, full of purpose, confident of its power and ability, unafraid to risk or change, willing to go the extra mile for each other.

I have not greatly concentrated in this speech on what areas of business development we should focus on. That is simply because I believe if the government concentrates on the foundations the market will do the rest.

I believe the Government must put strong foundations in place. We should ensure the back office is better, faster, more proactive and professional than those of competing countries. We should ensure that our company law is user friendly, our tax rates and conditions are attractive to both companies and individuals, our information and communication technology infrastructure is world class and both Enterprise Ireland and the IDA which I believe should be immediately amalgamated are firing on all cylinders. In short, Irish businesses and entre-preneurs and foreign companies and individuals who invest in this country should have immediately at their disposal the best playing pitch we can give them supported by the best backup team we can provide. We need a team that Ireland and Brian Cody would be proud of.

The speech was received well but with some curiosity. As I mingled with participants afterwards, I was complimented on delivering a straightforward assessment that, by and large, people agreed with. I have to admit, however, that there was some shock in the room that a politician would speak so openly about these matters. Two days later, on the Sunday, Eamonn and I met at Baldonnell aerodrome to fly to a ministerial meeting in Brussels. I noticed that Gerry Monks was giving me strange looks. As I settled down for the flight and I began to read the paper, I realised why.

My comments to the Beverage Council's annual conference had been reported by Brendan O'Connor in the *Sunday Independent*. O'Connor pointed out that I was not a 'maverick' and that it was a reflection on what was wrong with politics in this country that my 'common sense' attitude to reform of the public service would be regarded as somehow revolutionary.

At lunchtime the following day, the Civil, Public and Services Union (CPSU) held a meeting in Dublin to debate and pass a motion that called on me to withdraw my 'outrageous and wholly unjustified attack on his work colleagues in Enterprise, Trade and Employment and the wider civil and public service'. They also called on the Taoiseach and the Tánaiste to confirm that my comments 'do not reflect Government policy and that he be required to retract his statement or be asked to stand down from his post as junior Minister'. The CPSU deputy secretary general, Eoin Ronayne, said: 'You can't have a Minister make comments that undermine social partnership and get away with it.'

On Tuesday, 16 September, at the launch of Mid-West Regional Engineering Skillnet at the Castletroy Park Hotel in Limerick, asked by reporters whether I would withdraw the remarks, I said I would not under any circumstances and that I stood over everything I had said. I was taken aback by the fact that I was being asked to withdraw my opinion at the behest of a union.

Pressed by the media at an event in Galway, Brian Cowen said that I was indicating 'some personal views'. 'They are not the Government's views,' he said. 'The Government has indicated that the public sector reform programme is an important part of what we need to do to deal with the situation.'

Behind my back, the union and the Tánaiste met. All sorts of demands were made. Commitments were given by the Tánaiste that I would withdraw some of my comments, I later found out from the union. When I heard this, I insisted that the union should meet me. Time passed. I refused to withdraw anything I had said and then a meeting was finally arranged.

The meeting on 4 December was attended by Eoin Ronayne, CPSU shop steward Betty Tyrrell Collard, Eamonn and I, with an official to take the minutes. I explained my position and reiterated my beliefs. We had our exchanges and I said my door was always open. The official was to write the minutes and agree it with both parties. The minutes were never produced. I am aware that two of my staff were approached by the union. Without reference to me, one refused to join and the other did not renew their membership.

It is extraordinary that a speech based on common sense, from the point of view of someone with a practical approach to life and to politics, is regarded as heresy. It is even more extraordinary that the priority of a trade union representing employees of the State should interfere in such a political manner. The negative reaction to the speech was almost entirely contained to my Department, driven by one official who later admitted to me that she had not read the entire speech but just the extracts that had been reported in the media. Those who responded negatively got most of the media coverage but there was a large silent majority who responded very positively.

I received hundreds of letters, emails and messages from people across all sections of society, including many from within the public service—some at senior level. There were even letters from civil servants suggesting areas for reform and outlining examples of bad practice. They agreed with my position and urged me not to give up.

I cannot be true to myself or the people I represent if I merely walk out onto a stage and deliver, without personal involvement, a script prepared by someone else that simply reflects the Department's view. The country demands much better than this. We need change and a dynamic approach with new political structures and the opportunity for alternative voices to be heard. This differs from Brian Cowen's approach to leadership. He demands loyalty above all, promotes and sustains tribalism and resists change, preferring what I have heard him refer to as 'ground-hurling'.

Chapter 12 ～

｜BUSINESS AS USUAL?

When he was first elected as leader of Fianna Fáil and Taoiseach, despite nagging doubts, I had great hopes that the mantle of power would transform Brian Cowen and release the potential he undoubtedly has. His strong intervention late in the 2007 general election campaign had been a big factor in Fianna Fáil's success and I was looking forward to change, a new approach and strong leadership. This did not happen. The Fianna Fáil parliamentary party was waiting for a call to arms and a plan. It got neither. Our great white hope had become our great quiet hope. Brian Cowen, faced with big challenges, became a gloomy and sometimes surly political presence.

As I indicated earlier in this book, I think Brian Cowen is more a believer in the status quo than he is in the transformative power of politics. When forced to choose he will go no further than compromise. A review of his ministerial career as Tánaiste and in the departments of Labour; Energy; Transport, Energy and Communications; Health and Children; Foreign Affairs; and Finance show that he largely follows the official line and takes 'best advice'.

Instead of starting to clear the decks by issuing a full apology for the fact that Fianna Fáil had made many mistakes during the Celtic Tiger years and outlining his plan for the country, he became defensive and made matters worse. Brian Lenihan took the only sensible political course and bravely faced the facts and the people, saying that he had the Taoiseach's full support. That may be true, but what the Taoiseach didn't have was Lenihan's charm, courage or leadership and that has been reflected in every opinion poll taken since.

The Taoiseach's response to a rapidly changing situation and a disintegrating economy was neither sure nor sound. The public could see that the reform, change and leadership they were expecting and demanding were not being delivered and Fianna Fáil's popularity was dropping like a stone, as was Cowen's, and the public mood was becoming very negative.

Over in the Department of Enterprise, Trade and Employment, I was under concerted pressure as more and more organisations wanted and pressed for a positive response to the crisis. The mood in the Department had not changed appreciably and no action was being taken to co-ordinate a response—one would have expected meetings involving senior civil servants and all ministers in the Department regarding the co-ordination of policy, initiatives and actions across the Department. That did not happen or I wasn't involved, and I should have been.

The Department was central to Government's plan to help the economy. It does not generally interact directly, but it has the administrative, supervisory and policy-making role over State bodies that are hugely important to the country's success.

There was no reaction. Businesses large and small across the economy were in distress and it didn't look to me like the Department was going to burst onto the scene anytime soon. On top of this, I was getting frustrated about the fact that suggestions I was making were getting no response.

Had there been meetings between officials and ministers within the Department and with the Government with all ministers, including juniors, attending they could have been brought to the table for discussion. I am only saying that they might have been worth considering, but there was no forum for discussing initiatives or suggestions, mine or anyone else's.

When you are in deep water in a sinking boat you consider

every worthwhile suggestion and act swiftly if you think it will work. I began recording them and, because I had lost confidence in the system, began following up with letters.

On 21 November 2008, I put a number of ideas to the Taoiseach at a meeting of the Fianna Fáil parliamentary party.

One idea was €500 million from the National Treasury Management Agency to fund a soft business loan scheme for the city and county enterprise boards. On my own initiative, I had already spoken to the agency's CEO, Michael Somers, about this and he told me that the scheme was worth considering. Nothing happened. I spoke to Mary Coughlan about this, wrote to Brian Cowen, copied to his constituency office, on 18 February 2009 and wrote to Mary Coughlan on 12 March. Nothing happened.

Changes were needed to the State's approach to EU procurement rules because Irish companies were losing out due to the State's overcommitment to those EU regulations. Considerable sums were being spent on procurement, with some contracts going outside the State. Unlike countries such as France and Germany, we were not splitting the contracts to bring them within the value at which EU-wide tendering is required, which would keep the work in Ireland. I had made a submission to the relevant Minister, Dr Martin Mansergh, regarding the matter, raised it at a parliamentary party meeting and included it in my letter of 18 February to Brian Cowen. No reply.

I know nothing has been done, because when we had representations from the SME sector before the Lemass Group in June 2010, they were still complaining, incidentally proving the worth of that forum.

It is more than disappointing that no action has been taken on a matter where action is easily taken. Politicians or officials seeking cover on this behind EU rules cut no ice with me. Our national interest is at stake and the big boys are already playing the game. Only laziness or incompetence can be keeping Ireland on the sidelines.

Foreign investors in Ireland and Irish businesses were complaining about the level of commercial rates, development and other local charges being demanded of them. I discussed this with a number of officials in the Department and we then compiled a well-argued three-page letter to the Minister for the Environment and Local Government, John Gormley, recommending a three-year moratorium for commercial applications. No answer received.

On a trip to Moscow, I saw how efficiently our embassy, Enterprise Ireland and the IDA interacted. It led me to believe that throughout the world we should have an Ireland House for these two agencies, which frequently live apart, and a shared brief to promote all things Irish. Indeed, I suggested that Enterprise Ireland and the IDA be amalgamated to concentrate effort and save costs and I continue to believe that is what we should do.

After a trade mission to China, Japan and Dubai and a conversation with a representative of the Taiwan Government, I was convinced that Ireland should strongly enter the market for foreign students wishing to learn English. I knew one of the difficulties was that economic immigrants sometimes used this avenue to gain entry to the UK and Ireland, but it is a huge market and we have too little of it. I had no doubt that between my Department and the Department of Justice we could devise a system that would help increase our share and limit the scope of the abuse. In my letter to Brian Cowen of 18 February I raised this proposal and enclosed documents relating to it. No answer.

Again, this beggars belief. The UK earns £2 billion a year from foreign students. It isn't just the teachers that are employed. It is the office space and flats rented, the money spent on living costs and the tax earned from profits. It is also about the fact that many foreign students will be ambassadors for Ireland in their home countries. It is such an easy service to develop, with some foundation already in place, that it is ridiculous that we are dragging our feet.

The Irish Exporters Association came to me regarding a proposal, similar to a French scheme, that would help us with export credit insurance, a sterling stabilisation fund and a stimulus proposal. Their proposal had considerable merit. No action.

I raised many other matters that deserved attention and debate: transferring local planning officers underutilised due to the downturn to An Bord Pleanála to clear backlogs; the development of the horse industry in China; the provision of an interactive website for the Department—the current site is nothing like I proposed; funding and empowering county enterprise boards to enable them to grant small loans to micro-businesses and the SME sector; a forum for the SMEs; the trouble NERA was causing to the catering industry and so on.

The suggestions may not have been recession-beaters but they were worthwhile and deserved discussion and at least the courtesy of a reply so that I could deal with the people involved. Lack of engagement damages the Government's message that it is there to help. It was also causing me to question what I was doing in this pool of inertia.

Within the Department, I was having difficulties too. Civil servants take long-term views of what they do, but the trouble often is that having finally arrived at a decision they take a long time implementing it.

Neither the Minister nor the senior management in the Department were any help. They didn't seem to grasp the urgency. For a politician with a small business background the indecision and lack of enthusiasm was incredible.

Obviously, my proactive approach and my attempts, some-times successful, to shake off the departmental shackles and probe the system were not going down well within senior levels in the Department. However, among middle management and junior levels I think I had more support and I certainly got more help, but that was limited by the dead hand of the hierarchical culture.

Certainly, some officials were beginning to understand and respond to the fact that I did work hard and was not difficult to deal with.

Politically, I was on the edge. My Minister, Mary Coughlan, and Brian Cowen were showing, by their lack of engagement with me, that they did not approve of my desire to embrace the Civil Service rather than allow it to embrace me. Having served most of their time, untested, on a wave of good fortune, I don't think they were finding it easy to adjust and they didn't need me snapping at their heels. On the other hand, I didn't want to be sitting on mine.

I have no doubt Brian Cowen is personally a nice man and good and intelligent company, but you need to be more than nice and gregarious when you are leading a country, a point that Enda Kenny and Eamon Gilmore need to take on board. Enda Kenny leads a party torn apart and Gilmore a party that is torn between Leinster House and Liberty Hall. In Government, they will tear one another apart, another reason why Fianna Fáil needs a leader with ability, determination and a plan to take the helm now.

The fact is that I didn't start standing up to Brian Cowen or anyone else in 2004. I started to stand up in Kilkenny around 1996. Nothing I have seen, heard or done between then and now has convinced me that, in important matters, once you are sure of your course, there is any other alternative.

During my time in the Department, the full complement of junior ministers was summoned to Government Buildings twice. On the first occasion we were met by Brian Lenihan, on the day he delivered the 2008 Budget, to be informed of a reduction in our salary and expenses. I expected this, as I knew from listening to the SMEs that the economy was about to take a major hit. The second time we met was to be told by Brian Cowen that we all had to resign to allow him to appoint a new team of 15 instead of 20. When I reminded him at this meeting that gatherings in Government Buildings were never about good news, he didn't seem to appreciate the point or the humour.

Immediately after the meeting, I tendered my resignation and thanked the Taoiseach for the opportunity to serve. The resignation was effective from 21 April 2009.

The night of 21 April 2009, I was told by impeccable sources close to the Government that the Tánaiste had told Brian Cowen that it was her or me and insisted I should not be asked to serve again and, I had no doubt, she had the full support of senior civil servants and the unions. Cowen, essentially, chose the status quo and loyalty over ability and I was not re-appointed.

The fact that I had not been re-appointed generated a certain amount of media attention. Fine Gael's Leo Varadkar said in an interview on RTÉ television that I had been sacked for doing my job and many in Leinster House were genuinely shocked. But that's politics.

In interviews in the local and national media, I tried to hold a reasonable line, but it was difficult to explain away the perception abroad that I had suffered not for my work but for my independence at the hands of tribal politics. I understood that the line I had taken might get me into trouble and that was a price I was prepared to accept. However, there was clearly a will to rub salt into the wounds.

I discovered that the visitors' book in the Department, which is signed by all of those who attend meetings there, was being trawled to determine who I had been seeing. Naoise Nunn's name, thought perhaps to be damaging because he had been employed in a professional capacity by the Libertas organisation, was shown to the media, as was that of David McWilliams, to encourage the view that I was running some sort of subversive operation or trying to upstage the Minister. None of it is true. One or two other moves also took place, which, while they didn't relate directly to me, were unpleasant reminders of the power of Big Brother.

At a meeting with Brian Cowen when I explained this he simply passed it off as the work of the 'Praetorian Guard'! He didn't look too interested in putting a stop to it. Who was the Emperor and where were his clothes?

This is why so few politicians challenge the departments. They risk having co-operation quietly withdrawn or a whispering campaign started against them, actions that this book will almost certainly encourage. Furthermore, they will get little help from ministers who, by and large, have too much to lose themselves and maybe are already institutionalised. And slowly politics sinks in the estimation of the people.

No matter what Mary Coughlan thought of me, the authority of the office should have been protected and the spinners told to stop. But that depends on what a Minister believes about the authority of his or her office.

I decided to act. I don't like being bullied and I had seen the State steamroll too many people. I wasn't going to allow it to happen to me and, having encouraged others to do it, I had to stand up myself. I accepted an invitation to appear on 'The Late Late Show' with Pat Kenny, who initially seemed to have difficulty understanding that I had told my Minister she wasn't up to the job. I had, but her trouble was that she had put herself in the hands of senior officials in the Department and, like Brian Cowen in Finance, was 'relying on best advice' from those who, in my opinion, were not handling the financial crisis at all well.

The Department of Enterprise, Trade and Innovation needs to be reconfigured, perhaps under a committee combining representatives of Government and experienced business leaders, like Gerry Robinson, Peter Sutherland and Michael O'Leary (if he leaves his tank of testosterone outside the door) and others, including representatives of unions and the public service who have a genuine desire to see the country recover and succeed. They could use it as a testing ground for better organisational and human resources practices, with the intention of creating a public service centre of excellence that could show the way to reform, recovery and change and set new standards throughout the rest of the Civil Service: a model that could be replicated in, for example, a HSE hospital or the public administration of a county.

We fear radical steps so much in this country that we make radical mistakes trying to avoid them. We move from pulling something out of messy, but flexible, mire and, instead of washing it down and considering what the fault may have been, we get angry and set it in a bed of new inflexible concrete rules, which will cost a fortune to shift. We should consider human errors carefully and proceed to rectify them slowly. The method I am suggesting does exactly that—it tests and establishes trust in a small part of the system before moving on to something bigger.

Humanity is messy, flexible and very inventive. You can, for instance, spend fortunes dealing with a few rascals, which would be better spent encouraging their offspring onto a different path. The Jesuits have it: the lesser evil for the greater good. The point I am making is that using a sledgehammer to crack a nut is not sensible and can be expensive.

I know the unions would put up resistance but they must now abandon old ways and help build a better Ireland. A reformed public service helping to drive a successful Ireland could be growing instead of creaking. It would be positive for their members, the country and the unions themselves. Will they buy this or any other radical reform? Look at *Animal Farm*: Not as long as Boxer keeps contributing and the organisers sit with their feet up in Farmer Jones's house!

Back on the backbenches, surrounded by colleagues who do not believe Cowen can, but hope he will, someday, take the party and the country onto a path of success, I could watch business as usual operate within Fianna Fáil and the Government. It wasn't encouraging.

Fianna Fáil was and remains in disarray with only Brian Lenihan and a few other senior ministers putting up a fight. Cowen stays while others wait too long to decide what action they are going to take, in their own interest and that of the country and

the party, regarding the leadership. The feeling in the parliamentary party meetings is nothing like the spin coming out of
them. The weatherman who predicts rising tides is now more
important than the leader who waits for them. We get a few talks
on loyalty, sticking together and 'Up the Republic' but no plan.

Having seen all the leaders who went before him as far back as
Lynch in action, I just couldn't take it. Without support, but in the
hope of encouraging action within the parliamentary party, I
publicly called on Brian Cowen to go. He has permanently lost his
authority in Fianna Fáil and polls had the public giving him an
approval rating of below 20 per cent. When no alternative willing
to throw his or her hat in the ring appeared, nothing happened.
The troops stayed 'loyal' behind Cowen, bravely facing the fact
that in less than two years his leadership will take us to a Little
Bighorn.

Out of office, I turned to an idea that I had promoted in Bertie
Ahern's time, and against which he had moved quickly, if
unfairly—the Lemass Group, named after a man whose pragmatic approach and commitment I very much admire. The
Lemass Group is not meant to be an attack on the leadership; it is
a forum for discussion that encourages backbenchers to
investigate for themselves and form their own opinions rather
than receive them through the filter of Government. It springs
from my belief that a party or an organisation that encourages
active involvement and independence of thought is stronger and
more capable of change and renewal than one bound by the
doubtful bonds of blind loyalty and adherence to the rules of a
collective.

There have been attempts to discredit the group by those of
Cowen's supporters—although, publicly, not Cowen himself—
who still remain tied to party totem poles, but they have failed.
The group grows stronger and I hope it will remain permanently
a forum that will encourage debate and increase confidence
among backbenchers, and will remind them we came through the

door of Leinster House with a mandate from the people. That requires us to do more than just follow the Government's lead.

The last parliamentary party meeting before the summer recess of 2010 heard yet another challenge, this time from Noel O'Flynn, relating to the policies and direction of the party under the leadership of Brian Cowen. At this meeting I spoke and dealt with the Lemass Group. Brian Cowen moved quickly to suggest that he would accept the group and include it in the parliamentary party structure, but that was simply an attempt to institutionalise the group and draw its teeth. Now that it is successfully generating interest and requests to appear before it from many outside organisations, it should remain an independent body run by backbenchers for backbenchers.

At this meeting, Brian Cowen said he does not play games. I don't accept this position. In fact, it is his game-playing within the tribe that has caused a lot of tension. 'His way or no way' is not an inclusive way to conduct the business of Fianna Fáil.

In all my dealings with ministers and Government, I have never been personal. My objective is to be heard and to contribute to policy. I am prepared to accept that I am wrong or to bow to a better position. Unfortunately, there is no two-way debate and it is damaging the country and the party.

In looking to the next election, the question for Fianna Fáil is how many seats it could win with Brian Cowen as leader and if the numbers couldn't be increased if a new leader was in place with a new team and an agenda of reform and action. I still believe that a new leader and a new team is the only option, but it is also essential that a clear set of modern, dynamic, reforming policies will be there too.

Fianna Fáil has been weakened by too many years in coalition, perhaps because no leader has redefined its core values and promoted new ones. It is time to do that because the question of what Fianna Fáil now stands for is a legitimate one. But Brian Cowen is only a symbol of where we were, not a driver to where we should go. What is his plan? Does he have a strategy? The problem isn't just communications. You have to have a message or a policy to communicate. I don't think he does.

Since Brian Cowen became leader Fianna Fáil lost 80 seats at local government level, in an election that he ran from a helicopter. Unless strong action is taken, we will lose many more councillors, senators and TDs in two years' time, making it difficult for the party to retain critical mass.

But that is a battle yet to come and we should prepare for it and be led into it by a new leader, a radical reformer who redefines our philosophy and our core values and places his or her vision for the country confidently before the people. The people are demanding Quality Ireland, a country that strives for excellence in everything it does, including politics and public service. They want, through local government, to be put back at the heart of our democracy. They want leaders they can trust, goals they can believe in and a better, fairer future for all.

The challenge facing Fianna Fáil, indeed all political parties, and leaders in trade unionism, the public service and professions and businesses is that the Irish people do not want 'business as usual' anymore. They want a new Republic.

Chapter 13 ～

⌐THE WAY FORWARD

Ireland is currently experiencing a deep bout of depression, part of what Elisabeth Kubler-Ross identified as one of five stages of grief. It is the one that follows denial, anger and bargaining, after which there is acceptance before we move forward again. Following years of rapid growth and plain sailing, some of it now acknowledged as unsustainable, Ireland hit the rocks about three years ago, but we had been sailing far too close to them for far too long. The adjustment has been severe as people's incomes fall or they lose their jobs altogether. Debt built up in the roaring Celtic Tiger years is now becoming a millstone around the necks of many people and is causing great distress, anxiety and, in some cases, the breakup of families. We need to do more to acknowledge that Ireland is not just an economy—it is a society too.

We have spent a great deal of time in this book looking back. But that is essential. Too often, and it is a great pity because it manipulates our natural impulse to be optimistic, we are told that the past is the past, we have to move on, we are where we are, and must look to the future. In fact, I am sure that one of the, no doubt, many criticisms that will be made about this book will be that I spent too much time dealing with the past.

Sportspeople understand why the past is important. They spend endless hours analysing and discussing videos of their past performances and those of the team they are about to meet. They know they will move forward only when they eliminate the kink in the swing, the trouble with the backhand or the teamwork of the forwards. Then they take another tiresome step and they practise the new technique until they drop.

We have looked at past performance, are experiencing the pain and disappointment of a setback, but we know what went wrong and it's time to pick ourselves up, put the lessons we have learned into practice and start building a new Republic. What should Government do now?

I make no apology for the lengthy sad read you have had up to now. But do not doubt that it is the future that interests me and I want this country to be a winner. I have already used the example of the Kilkenny Senior Hurling Team which, I hope, will have won a fifth All Ireland title in a row by the time this book is published, and if they do not, it will not be for want of trying. They have everything it takes to win: skill, determination, ambition, team spirit and a manager, Brian Cody, who removes obstacles, confronts problems head on, picks the best 15, irrespective of what club they come from, and demands performance. That is what governments are elected to do.

I think few historians would argue with me when I say all institutions, states and ideologies have their time not because they are not intrinsically good, but because they become instruments of power and, ultimately, abuse. As Voltaire says: 'By their turn, every land has reigned over this world, by laws, through arts and, above all, by the sword.'

While, in the long run, we may be unable to prevent history repeating itself, we can at least try to defer the collapse for as long as possible or minimise its effect. That means embracing change, encouraging discussion about radical ideas and protecting the freedom of the individual. It also means balancing rights with responsibilities.

Most modern businesses throughout the world have embraced this concept. In his book *The Tipping Point* Malcolm Gladwell highlights the American company Gore-Tex, which divides up its product lines so that each can be housed in units comprising no more than 150 people. It has discovered the benefits of Dunbar's number, which suggests that this is roughly the number at which people reach a happy social balance, with social pressure at all levels rather than rules keeping people in line and fulfilled.

There will be those who say this is a cynical manipulation of human beings for profit. If it is, it is a happy cynical manipulation because the company's workforce is remarkably stable and content and the company itself is hugely successful. In any case, we are all driven by self-interest, hopefully enlightened and, frankly, the workers at Gore-Tex seem to me to have a much better environment than many in our public service labouring under workplace practices and thinking that belong to the Middle Ages and a management unwilling or unable to change the old order.

To bring about the new Republic that our people are demanding we have to change the State we are in by encouraging the people in it to embrace new ways. I suspect that will be more easily done from the bottom up than the top down. High priests tend to defend false gods to the death, because their lives depend on it. How then can we promote change?

REAL SOCIAL PARTNERSHIP

The time has come for public sector workers to have the same terms and conditions as their private sector counterparts. I am not suggesting that those already employed should lose benefits already agreed, but no one entering the Civil Service from now on should have a job for life or, indeed, anything other than the pay and conditions that apply in the private sector. Of course, for this to happen unions will have to abandon the unequal system they now support with the help of compliant governments.

All professional positions within the public service should be filled by fully qualified professionals. I don't mind if scholarships are provided by the Government to assist public servants to achieve these. Promotion to senior management level should be restricted as soon as possible to those with degrees or with the in-depth experience and attitudes necessary to convince a stringent interviewing board of their competence. These interviewing boards should comprise external human resources professionals, psychologists and, hopefully, on a pro bono and rotating basis, members and former members of boards of large Irish companies, with a minority of public service or political representatives.

The practice whereby public servants without any HR qualifications interview one another must stop immediately. It is incestuous, unprofessional and a ridiculous example of ego inflation. The fact that someone is a senior civil servant or, indeed, the managing director of a business, does not mean that they are good interviewers and very often they are not. Interviews should be left, principally, in the hands of objective professionals.

If you ask the public service how many people they have with third-level qualifications you will be provided with surprising figures. That is because the definition of 'third level' is very broad and it includes engineers, whose degree level or competence I am not questioning. However, the real question is, excepting engineers and officials in the Department of Foreign Affairs—a law unto themselves—how many BAs, MAs and Ph.Ds are there among our top 200 civil servants? Degrees or even Ph.Ds are not the be-all and end-all but they are a standard of excellence, albeit now diminished, and, like professional interviewers, a good place to start.

Essentially, our public service needs to have some business steel and experience injected into its backbone. At the highest levels, it is already complacent and is becoming mediocre. And that inadequate standard is slowly working its way through our State organisations. We will never have the back office this country needs unless we take some steps now to train or attract the best brains we can get and give them the opportunity to put what they know into practice.

When there is free movement of labour between departments within the public service and unrestricted movement at all times between the public and private sector, we will be well on our way to success and public service workers will be a lot happier.

There is no good reason for this not to happen. It is up to the Government and the unions—to all of us—to put on the green jersey and start playing a blinder for Ireland.

We need, cannot do without and must have a vibrant, creative, user-friendly back office. And we need happy, bright and energetic people running it.

Central to nearly every point made in this book are the trade unions. Nothing meaningful in this country happens without them. They are an essential pillar of our economy representing a huge number of people who would otherwise not have the means to press their case. The trade unions can stop this country from succeeding, or they can help make it great. But they need to change. Instead of being behind Larkin, they should be in front for Ireland.

They need to have a plan for the future that does not involve helping to keep their members dependent: well-paid security is no match for well-paid exciting, challenging and fulfilling work. Few psychologists or human resources professionals would agree with the way current union practices, generally, are promoting the social needs of their members.

It is essential, therefore, that the Government calls in the unions and asks them to grasp the moment, indeed it is vital that they do so. It would make a big difference if they began a sustained, careful and clever management of reform and change. I believe in a very short period of time it would pay dividends for the unions themselves, their members and the country. I am asking a radical movement that has become culture bound to break loose, return to its roots and renew itself to help this country face the future. If the unions do not do this, the Government must challenge them because the constant compromises that have marked labour relations in this country for the past 10 to 15 years must stop.

As usual the first step towards success is a willingness to change. If our political, business and trade union leaders can come up with a radical, vibrant new model, we will be well on our way. If they do not, we will be left behind.

PUBLIC SECTOR REFORM

The machinery we are using to run this State is obsolete, slow and tired. The public and many civil servants themselves are calling for a modern, efficient system that gives satisfaction and a sense of achievement to those who operate it and a speedy, friendly service to those who use it.

Earlier in the book, I proposed a Minister for Public Sector Reform with a seat at the Cabinet table and a remit to work across all departments to deliver the transformation that has long been promised but not delivered. We also need an infusion of fresh blood to begin to change the embedded culture. In order to achieve this, we need to reform the way we recruit public servants.

We need to provide much better quality and specific training for civil servants that reflects best international practice so Ireland can become an engine of economic expansion. We need to release the potential of people to perform at the highest level. Public sector reform in a real meaningful way is now urgent. Numbers need to be reduced across departments in the middle to senior management area. There are simply too many employed in every sector of Government and this was confirmed by the McCarthy and McLoughlin reports. There are more than 800 quangos and State agencies. That number needs to be substantially reduced and the responsibilities for those remaining brought under the control of the Dáil.

I think that once the State labour market is freed up and the benefits begin to flow into the economy, the overstaffing left after voluntary redundancies and natural wastage have taken their toll might be distributed across State and semi-State sectors. I say this because I do not blame public servants for where they are now. I blame governments and unions for letting them down.

Government departments should be driven by their ministers,

based on policies generally approved through the electoral process. Each Department should have to comply with a regularly audited NSAI standard. As stated previously, work has already been undertaken on this project by the NSAI. It just awaits the political will to implement it and there is no reason it could not be commenced immediately. The Government insists on standards in corporate Ireland, therefore, Government departments should have similar standards. Otherwise, it's a case of 'Do as I say, not as I do'.

A regulatory impact analysis should be conducted across all Government departments and agencies, including local government. Red tape and bureaucracy should be reduced drastically. Business leaders and, in particular, the SME sector, should be consulted. One size does not fit all. Government and local government should butt out of business as much as possible.

What infuriates most business people is the burden and expense that red tape and regulation places on their shoulders. The fact that it is put there by a State that is extremely careless about what it does with taxpayers' money while it chases them for peanuts doesn't help either.

Part of the problem is the one-size-fits-all nature of regulation. Large-scale abuse, like the underpayment of foreign workers in the construction industry, the genesis of the National Employment Rights Authority (NERA), has given rise to regulations that are being imposed on small and medium sized business without regard for common sense or appropriateness.

For instance, a NERA audit of a small business can result in that business having to repay shortfalls in minimum wage salaries going back years, resulting often in further pressure on the business and workers having to be let go, despite the fact that to help the business and to avoid losing their jobs they have agreed to accept less.

The question has to be asked: is it better for the State and workers, in circumstances like that, that they remain employed rather than on the dole? And it also has to be asked, is it right that the State should interfere with agreements that small business and their workers make between themselves?

POLITICS

Most people want a quiet life and there is nothing wrong with that. But, in a democracy, the quality of life depends on how well the country is run. That is or, more correctly, was in the hands of the politicians the people elected to the Dáil to represent them, make laws and oversee the administrative functions of the State.

Over the past 10 years or so, for various reasons, some to do with corruption, that power has slipped through the fingers of politicians into the hands of the unelected, who devised and were allowed to operate strategies to ensure they had to answer to the Dáil as little as possible. It is only in recent years that scandals in State and semi-State bodies, some of which I covered in this book, have revealed the true cost of lack of governance and accountability.

The people of Ireland now know the cost of not choosing their representatives with care and not paying attention and demanding good governance from those they elect. Their lives now are no longer quiet. It is a hard lesson. But what would happen if more people voted, took an interest in politics and insisted on quality representation and put a party into Government, which we will call 'New Fianna Fáil'? What might such a party do to meet the demands and expectations of the Irish people?

New Fianna Fáil would, I think, quickly form a committee with a majority of respected national figures—Colm McCarthy, Nuala O'Loan, Emily O'Reilly, Garret FitzGerald come to mind—some senior business figures and some politicians and civil servants, under the chairmanship of, perhaps Matthew Elderfield, the new banking regulator, who takes no prisoners and doesn't waste time. They would give that committee a month to set salary levels for

TDS and ministers and create a system for claiming expenses that was transparent, vouched and, above all, allowed no room for temptation.

The current system is run by politicians and civil servants and both benefit from it. No matter how honourable the participants are, that brings the process into doubt. Proper governance demands arm's length.

I believe TDS should be properly remunerated for what is a demanding profession, although Dáil sitting time should be extended. Many already do much more than 40 hours per week and should not be penalised because there are a few who behave badly. I also think that more committee work will have to be done and that should also be taken into account. Ridiculous window dressing, like fobbing (signing in and out of the Dáil) demeans the office and gives no credit to the work TDS do in their con- stituencies. I may be an extreme example, but I seldom do less than 60 hours a week, and I am not alone.

Again, we are back to the lesser evil, dealing with a few chancers, for the greater good, respect and reasonable reward for the diligent office holders. Furthermore, the people, who are now more informed than ever before, have a say through the ballot box. And the Dáil Committee on Procedures and Privileges has a significant say too.

That committee must be given much greater powers, so that it can deal severely with behaviour unbecoming, right up to requir- ing and forcing a TD or Senator to resign, and bringing in the Garda Síochána if illegality is discovered. I understand that may be difficult to achieve, but restoring and maintaining trust in politics and politicians is essential.

With New Fianna Fáil in place and salaries, expenses, con- ditions and sanctions agreed, the country might have to suffer a little pain while reality and the need for positive patriotic action were discussed and impressed on a number of national institutions.

The trade unions would have to be told that they had no option but to engage with modern best practice labour relations in the interests of the country and their members. Our accounting and legal practitioners would have to be told that their contribution to the banking crisis had not gone unnoticed and to get their houses in order or face tougher regulation. Senior public servants would have to be told that the days of internal audits, interviews and lack of professionalism were out and that leadership, excellence and external benchmarking were in.

Local government would have to be reconfigured so that power, politics and the people meet to their mutual benefit. I don't believe in publicly elected mayors. It's unnecessary and expensive window dressing and it involves the cost of an election. Instead, we should give existing mayors more power and responsibility, regionalise some services like planning and engineering and, above all, invest time and money, without bureaucracy, in social entrepreneurship.

For many years, influenced by the work of Bishop Birch and others in Kilkenny and from my experiences as a national politician, I have called for the introduction of new models for the social contract between the State and its citizens. You can call it 'social entrepreneurship' or, as David Cameron's Conservatives in Britain branded it, 'Big Society', but the message is the same.

I am greatly concerned that the State has created a whole society of marginalised people who are dependent on it for handouts but who are completely alienated from it. This culture of dependency cannot continue. A much better approach is to empower people in local communities to help themselves, gain confidence and grow. They will intervene, support and encourage the marginalised in their communities. Family resource centres are already demonstrating their work in this area.

We need professional community organisers, trained with the skills needed to identify local community leaders, bring communities together, help people start their own neighbourhood groups, and give them the help they need to take control and tackle their problems. Soft loans can be made from a community fund to help develop groups, charities, social enterprises and other non-governmental bodies.

New Fianna Fáil would, I am sure, take immediate action on a number of small Oireachtas reform measures, which would have immediate impact. Committees would be made more relevant to each Government Department and given the powers necessary to carry out their work effectively and in the public interest. The Dáil would update its Standing Orders to bring it into the twenty-first century and room would be made for genuine debate on the issues of the day with free votes and meaningful engagement from ministers. Parliamentary questions would be dealt with by a nominated senior civil servant in each Department with a guaranteed minimum response time for all TDs and an express system for ministers.

Bills before the Dáil would undergo a much greater degree of scrutiny and officials would be required to flag contentious sections. Currently, too many bills are guillotined with many amendments not being debated. This gives the ministers and their departments too much scope to disguise possible controversial issues, resulting in the devil jumping out of the unconsidered detail down the line.

I know and understand why governments are concerned about free votes in Parliament, but there are occasions in the lifetime of every Parliament when bills are introduced that are amenable to a free vote. A mature political system should be able to accommodate that. I have certainly voted for my party against my personal conviction—the ending of the dual mandate for instance—and will do so again, because the party system requires it. But there are bills where democracy would be best served by a free vote, particularly those not central to budgetary con-siderations that are the subject of diverse opinions in the country generally.

I am sure New Fianna Fáil would also have short, sharp meetings with many State and semi-State bodies, quangos and the rest, dismantling some, reducing others, slimming boards and cutting costs. There would be some whose worth would be recognised and whose help would be sought in getting the country back on its feet, because there is a hard core of efficient organisations in the system.

New Fianna Fáil would take no nonsense and wouldn't tolerate waste. And it would make the Dáil work, putting power where it belongs, but well under control. It would empower Dáil committees and ensure that they act in the interest of the people, allowing ministers to be called in and witnesses compelled to attend. It would have Dáil committees vet appointments to State and semi-State boards, which it had made more accountable to the Dáil.

The Public Accounts Committee would be strengthened and empowered to examine day-to-day expenditure instead of the retrospective system that exists now. Local government and county managers would be available to be brought before the committee for their audits. It should also have enhanced powers of compellability of witnesses, should be able to make recommendations for better practice and have options to take sanctions against those who have failed in their responsibilities. There are lots of examples throughout the world as to how this might work. Indeed, with Pat Rabbitte, I helped draft a report for the PAC to this end, which could be implemented easily with the political will.

The Seanad needs to be reformed but not abolished. The Taoiseach's 11 nominees should be vetted by a committee to ensure that they are bringing teeth and talent to the House. I believe that the Seanad could be a much stronger contributor to the legislative process providing it contains a reasonable number of strong independent voices.

I also believe that newly appointed ministers should go before the committees dealing with their departments. I would not give the committees the power to block appointments, but an early appearance before it would be an encouragement to incoming ministers to understand their brief and might also result in more careful selection. It might also restrict the number of ministers chosen because of geographic location, driven by political imperatives rather than by the departments' or the country's needs.

Mary Coughlan was transferred overnight from beef to balance sheet, a significant bridge for her to cross. It does, however, in its disregard for appropriateness, demonstrate that the belief that ministers are there to drive policy in their departments or are required to be anything other than a smiling face in a photo and the voice of the Department in the Dáil, controlled by a prepared script, has long since disappeared. A strong committee challenging ministerial appointments would go some way to redressing that balance.

Ministers would be picked for their abilities rather than the location of their constituencies, as sometimes happens. This would leave electoral success depending on national success. This would mean that ministers would have to deliver benefits across the country, controlled also by a requirement that they would have to stand back from decisions materially benefitting their own constituencies.

Certainly, there is a need to reform the Dáil and the Seanad and probably reduce numbers but let us see what both can do when they are energised and empowered, backed by a reformed local government and a public service that has risen to the challenge of fully participating in a drive to make a better Ireland.

Every time we talk about reform in Ireland, it has to be huge, involving committees and consultants. What is needed is small steps and simple improvements that can be checked and tested. Otherwise, the result is layers of additional bureaucracy, more regulation and little or no progress. But there is a purpose in this—mistakes are easily hidden and responsibilities avoided in the large rather than little.

New Fianna Fáil would surely start with State organisations, telling them to substantially reduce the red tape and petty rules that are stifling our SMEs and business generally, instructing them instead to engage, understand and co-operate, because common sense, confidence and trust go a long way in a State that is seen by all as straight and fair, which is not where we are at the moment.

Regulations would be put in place to stop the greedy and power-hungry on the top of the ladder from going through the ceiling. The State should be stopped from squeezing those in the middle for every euro just because it's easy, and those on the bottom of the ladder would be prevented from going through the floor because of lack of care or a shortage of respect, understanding and real support.

I don't believe it is sensible or fair to knock the rich. Ireland needs people who are driven to create and produce, and make money. They are needed, because they give employment and the majority pay substantial sums in tax. We need more entre-preneurs in this country and more well-paid executives of foreign companies locating here. Both have to be encouraged to stay and/or encouraged to come. There is tax competition between countries for their services and we have to compete. That said, we should have a firm regulatory regime that enforces rules and permits no nonsense.

At the other end of the social scale, there are people who simply want to live and some of them can't or won't work. A civilised society can understand and accommodate this. But we have to do much more to prevent some of these people falling into depend-ency. Far too little thought has been given to the growing alienation from society of large numbers of our people, many of whom now live in what are or are rapidly becoming ghetto estates around our towns and cities. That is a stain on how our society operates and if Government does not intervene in meaningful and clever ways, to help build self-respect and restore dignity in these lost communities, the troubles they are creating will continue to grow.

Between the extremes of great riches and great poverty are the people who work hard for a reasonable life for themselves and their children and who strive for a sensible work-life balance. They neither ignore nor abuse the State. They are good citizens who are squeezed by the State at every turn and they are now angry. Their children are having to leave the country, their own positions are increasingly insecure and they no longer believe in the worth of many of the pillars of our society. These people want a different republic that understands and acknowledges their worth and their needs. I believe they will, and should, make that very clear in the next general election.

But the great thing about New Fianna Fáil would be that the people of Ireland need to watch only the 100 from whom everything flows and by whom everything is regulated. What happens beneath them is their responsibility; monitoring State organisations; taking decisions that will affect their lives; ensuring money is collected, spent and accounted for properly and that the profit made, happiness, is spread fairly throughout the country. And if they don't deliver they can be sacked in, at most, six years. And they should be.

Actually, this is how huge multinationals with turnovers that dwarf Ireland's are run. They make mistakes from time to time and some go bad, but the vast majority of them are run by a board of less than 50 and, increasingly, they concentrate on keeping the people who work for them motivated and challenged and, of course, their shareholders happy. Should governments be any different?

We are a country of 4.5 million people. If we appoint the right politicians to our board in the Dáil, pay attention to what they do, refrain from penalising the many for the sins of the few, insist on integrity, passion and commitment and vote with our heads instead of our hearts, there is no reason why we cannot build a new Republic that we can all be proud of.